HOW TO
SAVE YOUR LIFE

HOW TO
SAVE YOUR LIFE

Sack your boss,
start your own business,
find your passion

Steve Carey and Susannah Bowen

A & C Black • London

First published in Great Britain 2009

A & C Black Publishers Ltd
36 Soho Square, London W1D 3QY
www.acblack.com

A CIP record for this book is available from the British Library.

ISBN: 9-781-4081-1214-4

This book is produced using paper that is made from wood grown in
managed, sustainable forests. It is natural, renewable and recyclable.
The logging and manufacturing processes conform to the environmental
regulations of the country of origin.

Design by Fiona Pike, Pike Design, Winchester
Typeset by Saxon Graphics, Derby
Printed in the United Kingdom by Martins the Printers, Berwick-upon-Tweed

CONTENTS

INTRODUCTION

¡Prefiero morir de pie que vivir siempre arrodillado!
(Better to die on your feet than live on your knees)
- Emiliano Zapata

Hello, and welcome to the rest of your life. The best of your life, too, if you get it right.

This is a business book not about tax returns and paperwork or business registration and compliance and all that good stuff, even though we talk about each of those at some point or another. Instead, it's a book all about you – about how you're feeling and how you'd like to feel. About how it feels to start a business and what you might expect to feel as you go through that process. About finding out who you are and what you can do and become – as opposed to what you believe your experience equips you to do.

We wrote this book because we wished we'd had it when we were launching our own businesses. In the years we've been at it, we've talked to thousands of business owners about their experiences and we've been struck by how often the same three themes come out, over and over again: freedom from being told what to do; the possibility of achieving a lifestyle that works for you – that elusive work/life balance; and just how good it feels when it's your own.

While we were writing this book, we interviewed hundreds of business owners in the UK and in Australia. They told us that they are now functionally unemployable; that, hard work though it is and at times financially challenging, they mostly don't regret it; that they've come to realise the critical importance of marketing; that tapping into your networks and having a supportive partner and a good 'dream team' on your side is essential to prevent loneliness, and that loving what you do and doing what you love is more rewarding than any other professional experience they've ever had or could imagine.

Despite what you may think, there are few natural born entrepreneurs. For most of us it's something that develops out of circumstance. You're looking for greater flexibility and a better lifestyle, to bring up the kids or to spend more time with them, and working for yourself offers the best opportunity to achieve those things. You're looking for something to keep you active and earning and a way of giving back to the community, as your mainstream corporate career comes to a conclusion and you downsize your job and, perhaps, your home. You've been inspired by someone you've met or bought from, or by an opportunity you've stumbled upon. The global financial crisis has led to your position being made redundant and you're considering working for yourself as a possibility. *Whatever the road you've travelled to get to this point*, you're now at the crossroads and you're looking for direction. We hope this book helps you find it.

We should say right here that we'll be disappointed if you agree with everything we say. Everyone's journey is different and we each see the view from a different place. Actually, for much of the time the two of us don't agree with each other, and for a fair proportion of the time (looking back at what we've written) we don't even agree with ourselves. Throw this book at the wall if it makes you feel better (it worked for us).

We thank our respective partners, Adrian and Helen, for their patience while this book kept us at our laptops. They know, as we cannot, what it's like to be partners to the self-employed; and we know, perhaps more than they, how important their support has been.

Most of all we thank the many, many self-starters, entrepreneurs and business owners who shared their stories with us in person, by email and by questionnaire. If we can't agree on everything that's in this book, we certainly don't expect them to. Their perspectives have always been stimulating and thought provoking, and we have loved hearing their tales of how they found themselves running their own businesses. In particular, we must thank, in strictly equitable order by forename: Alison Richardson, Richardson Associates, www.richardsonassociates.co.uk, Derbyshire, UK; Andrew Wozencroft, gardener, Aberdeen, UK; Andy Roy, NeXus Management

Solutions, www.businessadviser.com/roy-a.htm, Guelph, Ontario, Canada; Ashley Fernandes, Crossing Cultures, www.crossingcultures.com.au, Sydney, Australia; Bryn Bazzard, Quocom Ltd, www.quocom.biz, London, UK; Carel Venter, Centre for Synergy Development, www.csd.org.za, Cape Town, South Africa; Carl Gould, CMT International, www.CMTmentors. com, New Jersey, USA; Christine Spencer, Business Consultant, christinespencer@iib.ws, Guildford, UK; Danny Hancock, Business Improvement Solutions, Gold Coast, Australia; Dave Boulter, Boulter Associates Pty Ltd, www.boulterassociates.com.au, Sydney, Australia; Dawn Mancer, Marketing and PR Consultant, www.firestormpr.co.uk, Cambridge, UK; David Hollinger, Prime Business Group, New Jersey, USA; David Jenkins, TDnJ Business Consulting, www.tdnj.net, Georgia, USA; Elizabeth Arnold, The Really Effective People Company Limited, www. repcoltd.co.uk, UK; Eric de Diesbach, Platinum Advice, www.platinumadvice. com.au, Sydney, Australia; Eva Hussain, Polaron Language Services, www. polaron.com.au, Melbourne, Australia; Firdaus N. Kapadia, FNK Corporation, www.fnkcorporation.co.in, Nashik, India; Francoise Garnier, Garnier Marketing Pty Ltd, Melbourne, Australia; Frank Willems, At Ease BV, www. at-ease.nu; www.gerustondernemen.nl, Bladel, Netherlands; Garth Borgelt, Allsorts Consulting & Training, www.allsortsct.com.au, Queensland, Australia; Geoff Cutter, Melbourne Business Foundations, Melbourne, Australia; Hylton Barnes, MMC Sweden AB, Stockholm, Sweden; Jo Bryant, Occupational Therapist, www.cowork.com.au, Melbourne, Australia; Jo Rhodes-Lewis, Tangible Developments Ltd, www.tangibledevelopments. co.uk, Chester, UK; Johan Venter, JPV Business Solutions, Pretoria, South Africa; John Shaw, Beachcroft Consulting, Johannesburg, South Africa; Karen Dickson, Kinesiologist and Clinical Hypnotherapist, karen.dickson@ ayus.com.au, Melbourne, Australia; Les Stuckey, A3 Consulting & Coaching, www.a3cc.com, Alabama, USA; Luke Harvey-Palmer, Buzzle, www.buzzle. com.au, Sydney, Australia; Malcolm Parr, Bookkeeper, www. betabookkeeping.co.uk, Horsham, UK; Mary Honan, For Marketing Matters, www.formarketingmatters.com, Andover, UK; Michael Coleman, Cranbourne Music, www.cranbournemusic.com.au, Victoria, Australia; Michael Shefi, Michael Shefi & Associates, Jerusalem, Israel; Mike Lescai, Meerkat

Associates Pty Ltd, Melbourne, Australia; Paul Rattenbury, Business Consultant, paulrattenbury@iib.ws, West Grinstead, UK; Peter Borg, Peter Borg & Associates, www.peterborg.com.au, Melbourne, Australia; Raeleen Harper, Bowen Therapist and Clinical Hypnotherapist, Melbourne, Australia; Richard Ferguson, Web Enhancer, www.webenhancer.com.au, Melbourne, Australia; Robert Hamilton-Jones, Business Advantage International, www.businessadvantageinternational.com, Melbourne, Australia; Robert Sampimon, Sampimon Business Solutions, Byron Bay, New South Wales, Australia; Roger Powell, WhiteSpaces Management and Marketing Services, www.whitespacesmarketing.com, Melbourne, Australia; Rose Michael, Arcade Publications, www.arcadepublications.com, Melbourne, Australia; Sarah Day, Day One Business Services, www.dayonebusinessservices.com, Minneapolis, USA; Stan Sweeney, Guidepost Strategies, www.guidepoststrategies.com, San Antonio, USA; Stefan Wasinski, Consulting Well, www.consultingwell.com.au, Sydney, Australia; Stuart Hayes, Starnext, starnext.com.au, Melbourne, Australia; and Tony O'Reilly, Red UK, www.reduk.net, Leeds, UK.

Susannah would like to say that any mistakes in this book are Steve's, and Steve would like to return the favour.

Susannah dedicates her share of this book to her mother, who makes her days easier, and Jackie, who makes her days better; Steve dedicates his, with thanks, to lpd.

CHAPTER ONE

WHY EVERYONE'S LEAVING

1. Route one: you choose to leave

Once upon a time, it went like this.

You knew where you stood. You grew up, kicking a football in the street, jumpers for goalposts. (OK, maybe this wasn't you, but it was your dad. It was a man's world then.)

You worked hard at school. Your careers officer ridiculed your plan and told you to be sensible. So you were. You went to university. You joined a big firm in a small job. You did as you were told and they looked after you. You worked hard and got promoted. You worked hard and got promoted some more. Then one day they stood around you, gave you a round of applause, presented you with a clock, as if to mock you. Then you went home and dropped dead.

In Japan this is still pretty much the arrangement. And it's killing them – or rather, it's driving them to kill themselves: Japan has one of the highest suicide rates in the world.[1]

That was then. Now it's different. If you're 40, it's unlikely you are still working for the same company you went to work for when you left school or university. And if by some chance you are still working for the same company, it's very unlikely you will still be there long enough to collect a clock. Which means?

It means you're expendable.

Loyalty – a dead word?

Of course, it works both ways. If you're expendable to employers, then they're expendable to you too. You probably no longer feel the same sense of loyalty to your current employer that your father did, or any great obligation

---

[1] www.timesonline.co.uk/tol/news/world/asia/article4170649.ece

to work for them for the rest of your life, as your father used to. (It used to be a man's world, remember.) At least, not such a big obligation that you would refuse to consider an invitation to join another company – even a competitor – if they offered you a much better job, with much better pay and much better prospects. Or if you *do* feel such a sense of loyalty and obligation, then you are certainly unusual.

Which means? It means that the bond between employer and employee is weaker.

Meanwhile, you are working longer and harder than your parents did. That's because you're under pressure, and you are under pressure because your company is under pressure. (Americans lead the world in this respect: they get no statutory leave and take only about half as much time off as Europeans. It's the way of the future.)

This is not what we'd have predicted 20 years ago, when we used to think that increased prosperity would leave us free to do other things…not that increased prosperity would trap us like amber and we'd be squeezed harder and harder to meet our obligations. You are not only working longer, you're working harder, because about ten years ago your company sacked half its workforce and thought it wouldn't make much difference.

So let's recap and see if we've got this right. The money is better, but the pressure's greater, the loyalty's less, the work is harder and there's more of it.

Having fun? Not surprisingly, no – not all that much.

In fact, lately, you've started wondering whether it's worth it all. The commute. The pressure. The long hours. The insecurity.

So what happens next?

In the light of this depressing analysis, what are you going to do about it? Nothing, probably. That's what most people do. Or you'll look for another job which will turn out a lot like this one. And that's OK. Bye-bye.

On the other hand, you may still be reading this because you're made of better stuff. You've already tried doing nothing about it and that didn't work. Not surprisingly, nothing changed. Even less surprisingly, the feeling of dissatisfaction didn't go away but instead got stronger.

Now you've got to the stage where you can't suppress the feeling any more. Perhaps this is a little frightening. We don't blame you a bit, because you *should* be scared. You're growing out of the mould. You're becoming less useful to your employer. It may even have got to the point where your work has started to suffer. If it hasn't, it may well soon.

The bad news is, this really *isn't* going to get better by itself.

The good news is the rest of this book.

HOW TO TELL IF THIS IS TERMINAL

Try the following. It's guaranteed to tell you whether this restlessness is Just A Passing Phase That You'll Get Over. It comes in two parts.

The first part is to give yourself a break. Pretend, for one week, that the *only* thing stopping you from striking out on your own and sacking your boss is your decision to do it.

Forget, just for seven days, all the reasons why It Can't Possibly Work, Obviously. *Let the difficulties argue for themselves*, as Winston Churchill so wisely put it. Imagine not what your business would be or how you would pay the bills, but how you would *feel*. And, since you're letting the difficulties argue for themselves, envisage this as a success. You have lots of work; more work, in fact, than you can handle. It is good work, too: challenging, fun, lucrative. Your biggest issue is how to find time to handle all this work and not let anybody down.

How does that feel? How do you feel?

By the way, don't forget the boss. You don't have one. *You* are the boss. You drive past the golf course and the pub and the shopping mall not because you are on someone else's time, but because you are on your own time. Not because you are in a hurry to make money for someone else, but because you are in a hurry to make money for yourself.

Dream. Just for these seven days, really *dream*. Luxuriate in it. Wallow. Describe how it feels and what would be the one visible sign that this was your life. Would you be banking a thick pile of cheques, for example? Would you be celebrating a major deal with a bottle of champagne? Would it be going back to where you used to work and punching your boss in the head? How do you *see* this success? *Write down* how this feels. Keep a diary and make entries when you feel like it.

Then, at the end of this week, we want you to *forget all about it*. Put this book into a bottom drawer and, with it, all your notes. Pretend it never happened.

It's what happens next that will tell you everything you need to know, with crystal clarity.

Maybe you'll forget all about it. One day, months from now, you'll come across this book and some old scribbled notes you don't recognise, and you'll wonder what *that* was all about. 'What was I thinking?' you'll ask yourself.

Or maybe not. Maybe this week will actually have awoken something in you. You'll have scratched an itch and it will just have got worse – much worse. Now the damned thing won't go away, even if you want it to.

You know what? Either is good. That's the really great news: either outcome is absolutely fine. If you give this some head space and then find it just fades away, it was never meant to be. It's not for you. Excellent! You have saved yourself a lot of upheaval, heartache and disruption. You have almost *certainly* held onto a whole lot of money you might otherwise not have.

So too if it goes the other way. If you are unable to get this whole thing out of your mind and the itch becomes unscratchable, *congratulations*. It's early days, of course, but you are now on your way to a whole new and very thrilling chapter in your life. (By the way, don't worry too much about what we said back there about upheaval and heartache, and the money you'd lose. We only said that because you were kind of expecting it. It's all true, but you don't need to hear about it just yet. There'll be plenty of time later. In fact, forget we ever mentioned it – we rather wish we hadn't, now.)

So rejoice, either way, because *whichever* decision you come to will, by definition, be the right one for you. Embrace it, genuinely.

OK, since you're still reading, we think that you are definitely a terminal case. Congratulations.

You haven't chucked in your job just yet (at least we hope not, and if you have, don't blame us; it was your idea and if you'd asked us we'd have advised against it). But you are definitely at the stage where you want to think about this some more. Cool.

Well, here's the plan. We are going to give you some stuff to think about, and if it gets you going a little further, we can really start to get serious. Sound good? Right, let's get going. Skip the rest of this chapter and get on with Chapter 2.

2. Route two: you get no choice

For the past few pages we've been talking about someone who's finding working for The Machine harder and harder to stomach, someone who's got themselves to the stage of wanting to look into the alternatives a little more seriously.

Your situation is a bit different and, frankly, more common. It is not unusual these days to get chewed up and spat out by The Machine. This usually happens for one of two reasons:

1. **The Machine doesn't think it needs you any more
   (it may be right about this).**
2. **There's been some kind of a terrible mistake.**

The bad news is, whatever the reason, the result is the same. We hate to break it to you, but there's only about a 5 per cent chance that The Machine is ever going to realise what a terrible mistake it's made. And there's only about a 0.5 per cent chance that it's going to think that the mistake was so terrible that it calls you up and says, 'Look, there's been a Terrible Mistake. Would you be willing to consider coming back at all?' It's not going to happen.

Now we could try and tell you that this is really great news that's just been very, *very* cunningly disguised, and that in fact it might just turn out to be the best thing that could have happened to you. But we know you're not in the mood, so we won't. (Even though, actually, it may be.)

So there it is, and here you are. You reading this book may well be you doing some research, taking the chance to examine your options. Good. We thank you, and hope that over the next couple of hundred pages you'll find what you're looking for. In the meantime, pursue all options and consider all offers.

Two worlds

There is another world – a parallel universe – that you may hardly be aware exists. You know about Corporate World. You work for a big company, and maybe so do most of the people you know. It's a place of pressure, politics, targets and budgets, bonuses (in good times…remember them?) and savage cutbacks (round about now), strategic initiatives and corporatespeak. For many of us, this is all that we know.

Out there it's different. For one thing, it doesn't even have a name. For another, it's where a huge amount of the action takes place.

Surprised? How about this: around half of the economy *doesn't* take place in Corporate World at all. Just looking at the United Kingdom, independent businesses make up 99.9 per cent of companies, employ 59 per cent of the private workforce and make up 52 per cent of business turnover.[2]

Put it another way; there's a *lot* of action out there, outside of Corporate World.

This is the world of independent business, to give it one name. It is also sometimes called Small to Medium Enterprise (SME), though that is not a term we like very much since it focuses on size, or the lack of it. The real issue here is not size, but independence and entrepreneurship. So, for lack of a better name, let's call it Entrepreneur World.

And it goes something like this, if you can imagine it (it does take some getting used to).

You have an idea in your business for a product or a service. You do it. That's it.

That's it. You are the boss, and that's the point. If your idea stinks, you go broke and lose the house. If it hits, you get rich and buy a second one. You don't have to run your idea past anyone. If you have a passionate, burning belief in your baby, you go and do it.

Of course, you'd be utterly stupid actually to do it this way – to take no advice, to do no testing, just to rush right out there and do it. (Funnily enough that is the way it gets done a lot of the time, which explains a lot. But that's another story, which we address later in this book.) Any smart entrepreneur takes a lot of advice, does a lot of testing.

So the essential difference here *isn't* that Corporate World consults and tests before it acts. The essential, vital, oh-so-crucial difference is that in Entrepreneur World you consult and you test *because you want to.* So? So

---

[2] www.hm-treasury.gov.uk/d/pbr08_economicengine_2390.pdf

this: it's *your* baby, it's *your* decision.

At its best, Corporate World provides a wonderfully supportive and creative environment for individuals to develop new products and services. The trouble is that phrase, 'at its best'. If you have ever experienced Corporate World at its best, you will know what we mean. And if you are experiencing Corporate World at its best, what the hell are you doing reading this book? It is intended and designed for people who know what it is like when Corporate World *isn't* at its best – which, we venture to suspect, is actually most of the time.

There is one other vital difference between Corporate World and Entrepreneur World, and it's this. It's *yours*. So when you walk out of that meeting having just nailed the deal, guess who the cheque is made out to? *You*, that's who. (In fact it's probably made out to the name of your business, but you get the point.)

> **Running your own business is NOT for everybody. If it is for you (or you are committed to making it work), the rewards (both personal and professional) are limitless!** Carl Gould, CMT International

Imagine that. *Savour* that. Just for a second. It's *yours*. This is so immensely rewarding and invigorating an experience that we can't even really begin to describe it to you. The first time you witness someone writing a cheque made out to you, it's a little like a car crash; everything goes into slow motion and you wonder what on earth is going to happen, because something surely will, to stop pen hitting paper.

Of course, there is a downside to all this. We alluded to it earlier when we casually mentioned that if you fail, you go broke and lose the house. But let us repeat yet again those wonderful words of Winston Churchill: *Let the difficulties argue for themselves*. If you worried about what could go wrong, you'd never get out of bed in the morning, let alone strike out by yourself and start your own business. *A man's reach should exceed his grasp or what's a heaven for?*, as the poet put it (Browning actually, not Shakespeare).

Oh, and one other thing. Although that corporate you work for is now probably owned by thousands of shareholders or a venture capital mob, once upon a time, hard as it is to believe, it was certainly started by an entrepreneur – just like you.

Entrepreneurship, rather than capital, is the real mainspring of the economy. Want to have a crack?

YOU'RE TOLD WHAT TO DO

At last count, there were more than 143 new books on management published last year for every man, woman and child on earth. Your boss, it is believed, bought approximately 7 per cent of them.

It doesn't seem to be working, does it?

You know it, we know it and deep down even your boss knows it (or why buy all those books?): your boss stinks. A recent survey indicated that more than half of employees think their boss is 'totally ineffectual'.[3]

Now why is that? Is it because you are desperately unlucky, stuck with the World's Worst Boss? No, it's not that.

It's because corporate life stinks, and your boss is channelling stink.

Corporate World does three things that drive people nuts. In ascending order of likelihood to cause an aneurism, these are:

1. They tell you what to do

You are a manager with a department or, if you're lucky, a team. You like telling them what to do. You're good at it. That is one side of the coin. The other is that you have a boss and/or board who tells you what to do. And guess what? They are *terrible* at it. They have a whole other agenda that doesn't even nearly coincide with your part of the business. They don't see things clearly or, if they do, they don't see them in the same arrangement as you do. When things are going well they expect too much too soon, and when things are going badly they demand the worst kind of cost cutting. Frankly, they couldn't run a whelk stall, whatever a whelk is.

That's bad enough. But you know what's worse than them telling you what to do?

2. They *don't* tell you what to do

They do not give clear direction, they mudge and they fudge, they flip and they flop. They screw you around and then they blame you when it all goes wrong. Boy is that annoying.

---

[3] www.news.com.au/business/story/0,23636,22061383-462,00.html

And if not telling you what to do is even worse than telling you what to do, that's not the worst of it. Here's the worst of it:

3. They tell you what *not* to do

You know it will work. *You* know it will work. You *know* it will work. Every instinct, every fibre of intelligence and gut instinct tells you what must be done. There it is – an opportunity to be grabbed, or perhaps a danger of some kind that must be avoided, or in any case, some kind of action that you know must be taken.

And then they say no.

You should not have to put up with this, you tell yourself. You are better than this, you tell yourself. And you know what? You are absolutely right.

You know what else? It is not going to change. *After all, how come we know so much about how you're feeling?*

CHAPTER TWO

WHY ARE YOU READING THIS BOOK?

What surprised me? The level of commitment and passion it takes to succeed. If you don't have a real passion for the business you want to start then stay in the corporate world. Richard Ferguson, Web Enhancer

This chapter is about paths to feeling better about yourself. The main thing to remember is you don't have to feel like this. You really don't. The world is too fun a place for you to drag yourself off to work every day, wishing you were anywhere else.

What you're looking for here is something pretty special – a way of living that brings you what you need to make you happy. A job that does what you want. That's important, so let's say it again in bigger letters:

A job that does what YOU want
- not what your partner wants (though that's important too, and we'll come back to that);
- not what your Mum thinks you should do;
- not what your secondary school teacher implied you could, couldn't or should do.

This is all about you. Unlike your mum, partner and secondary school teacher (probably), you get to be one of those lucky people who leaps up in the morning and feels full of energy and says 'Yes! I get to go to work!' Wouldn't that be just gurt lush, as they say down Bristol way?

The downside of course is you have to figure out what this job is and go and get it. But with us on the team, that's a piece of cake.

How did you get here, anyway?

To build your future, we're going to have a look at how you got here in the first place. We want to look back as well as forward. We're going to get you thinking about the goals and ambitions you had for yourself as a child, a teenager, a winsome youth and a university student. Odds are that's when you were more passionate about your interests and loves, before cold reality set in and you started worrying about mortgages. If you can remember what floated your boat then, you might well find that it still does – just so far down that you've forgotten.

This is the single hardest bit about this whole setting-up-for-yourself idea: figuring out what you want to do. (Up until the point when you have to actually, you know, *do it*, that is. That's not exactly as easy as running a whelk stall either. But compared to dragging yourself out to do a job you hate, it's not so bad.)

By the way, if you're lucky enough to have an iron-clad idea of what you'd like to do with yourself, congratulations! And you get to skip this bit if you want and go straight to Chapter 3. On the other hand, be our guest if you'd like to do this anyway – it never does any harm to make sure you really are on the right path.

The YOU Questionnaire

Don't try and draw too many deep and meaningful conclusions from this. It is merely designed to get you reflecting and give you ideas.

We've left enough space in the book for you to jot down your answers as you work through it. And we recommend that you do so – it means your answers won't get lost. Unless you lose the book of course. Hell, buy another copy (and buy a spare, too). We need the royalties.

1. What did you want to be when you grew up?

• When you were really little, what was your dream job?

_____

_____

_____

_____

• Why? What was it that you loved about the idea of being a spy, or a firefighter, or an astronaut?

_____

_____

_____

2. Remember that point at school where you had to pick some options?

Usually these options were either stuff about words and books and languages, or more science-oriented. So…

• Why did you choose the path you did? Was it because you liked the subjects, or someone told you to, or you thought they would lead to jobs, or be easy?

_____

_____

_____

• What would have happened if you'd followed a different path?

_____

_____

_____

• What if you'd chosen subjects purely based on what you liked to do?

_____

_____

_____

• Has anything happened since to change your opinion of the pathway you took then?

_____

_____

_____

3. What happened after school?

Did you go to college or university or out to work? What drove your decisions? What other paths might you have taken?

_____

_____

_____

4. What was your first proper job?

Was it something you fell into, or part of your career strategy (a career strategy as a graduate? Yeah, *right!*)? Was it what you thought it would be?

_____

_____

_____

5. What job have you enjoyed most/least?

What did you like and what was dreadful?

_____

_____

_____

OK, keep all those memories churning about. Now let's put the real world on hold for a minute and think about dreaming. This is a bit hard to do – it might be the hardest thing in this part of the book, actually, and here's why:

We'd like you to put all your doubts and fears aside and just think about what you actually want for your life.

It's a big ask. Here are some tips on creating that space in your mind:

• Clear some head space

You can't dream with all the minutiae of day-to-day life banging around inside your bonce. So take a long walk or a jog or a drive; get out of your usual environment (home/work/the train that runs between the two) and let ideas run amok.

• Carry pen and paper with you – at all times

The best ideas come at unexpected times and you think, 'Oh wow, that's good! Must remember that,' and then you don't. So write them down when they pop up.

• Talk about your life and what you just maybe could do with it

To family, to friends, to complete strangers at bus stops. Bang on until people start backing away from you. The more you talk (and listen), the more new and old ideas come up and the more you can figure your way through this maze. It's not very British, this. But that's OK: you can do it if you really want.

Right, now let's go further into it and get down to some serious dreaming. We're going to work through some topics here and decide on the key attributes of your dream job. Take some notes as you go. This stuff is important.

About you

6. What are your interests?

What do you like doing? If you love golf or painting or kids or writing or lead-lighting, take it seriously at this point. After all, there *are* people who make a living doing this, so why not you? Somebody has to do it. No reason on earth at all why it shouldn't be you.

CASE STUDY

Eva Hussain, translation and interpretation

Eva was 18 years old, seven months pregnant and spoke not a word of English when she emigrated from Poland to Australia. Today she runs Polaron Language Services, a thriving translation and interpretation business.

'After I improved my English, I took a degree in computer programming, discovering along the way that I didn't really like the subject. In my first job at a telecommunications company, I took my first translation accreditation exam and gradually added to it to get to a professional level of interpreting.

'Then I went to work for a local council, until my boss told me I "didn't fit in" and "wasn't a team player". I walked out in shock and never went back. Thinking about what I had, I realised that I possessed a bunch of interpretation qualifications and that there was a lot of work translating Polish into English. So I registered with some companies as a contractor, and got down to it.

'I made some mistakes along the way. I discovered I didn't have business or financial training, and I burnt myself out rushing around everywhere. But when I checked out the competition, I started to realise that they lacked skills I had learned in customer service.

'Over time I built up a reputation, to the point where people were coming to me. I hired my first part-time person in 2002, when we were working out of home in our tiny converted utility room! Then we took over a bedroom, and then we moved out to these offices.

What do I get from it?
1. No bullshit! I'm working with real people and on real issues, and I get to filter what I do. No meetings, no Key Performance Indicators, none of that stuff you get in big business. That can be a negative too, because there can be a lack of structure.
2. I'm dealing with staff, and suppliers, and stress… but it's all mine to make or break. I'm my own decision maker, and I love that.

And what have I learned?
1. In the end, it all comes down to money. It's not about how busy you are – I used to get mad when my husband asked me how come I was working so hard yet not earning anything!
2. You have to be tough. If you're an assertive woman, you get called a bitch – but you face challenging issues and you have to develop your assertiveness skills, even if that doesn't come naturally
3. Love what you do, but give yourself some time off too. Take a break!
4. Get yourself a mentor. You're inside the bubble all the time, and you need someone with some outside perspective.'

7. Your skills

Now, what can you do? Can you sail a boat, assemble Ikea furniture, crochet? Can you write a report, analyse a spreadsheet, make a sale? Speak a foreign language? This might be a big long list – and remember that some will be things you learned to do at work, and others skills that you've picked up along the way. Both are important. Oh, and because this is a section on dreams, you're allowed to add skills you don't actually have but would love to acquire.

8. Your lifestyle

What hours would you like to work? Seriously. Susannah's dream job would be working about one day a week but being paid for full time (she has two young kids, you see); Steve's would be working full time but being paid for about five full-time jobs. Neither kind comes along particularly often, and perhaps your dream job doesn't either. So let's just agree on that bit and move on.

Aside from that, do you fancy early start/early finish? Are you a night owl or a morning lark? Night shift? Nine-to-five, like the song? Ten days on, ten days off? Short hours – ten till three? Three long days a week? School holidays off? Lots of travel? No travel at all? Whatever it is, figuring out what works best for you is a great starting point.

On the same theme, would you like to work from home? Some people love it and the lifestyle it brings. No commute! You get up and can sit at the computer in your PJs eating porridge if you want. Potter around, hang up washing in your lunch break, get to know the people who run your local shops. Work a bit, do home stuff, work a bit more – you can mix it up. No getting sweaty on public transport and when you knock off for the day, there you are – at home. No costs of running an office. Magic.

For others, working from home is a dreadfully bad idea. No separation! You get up and the computer calls and that's it, you're working. No lunch break without worrying about the washing, no work colleagues to chat to, no change in environment during the day – you can get cabin fever at home. Then you knock off for the day…and think of one more thing to do…and hop back in…and knock off again…and remember something else…and it never ends. *Blergh.*

Don't forget your family and the kind of lifestyle they might like you to have. If you've got young kids, flexibility in hours is probably key – to be there at the top and tail of their day. If your kids are in school, think about jobs that allow you time off in school holidays. If your partner works Monday to Thursday, try not to take a job that runs Friday to Monday, or your relationship may suffer.

Talk to him or her – make sure they're comfortable with the kind of lifestyle changes you're talking about. Even if they don't love the idea, will they support you while you give it a go?

Do you like travelling for work, or not? Or only if it's Hawaii and five star hotels?

[We interrupt this paragraph to bring you an important note: this exercise is about DREAMS. It's like brainstorming – park all the 'no way will that work' and 'that will never happen' and 'you can't get a job like that in a town like this' thoughts. If what you really and truly want for your life is to work two days a week as a taste tester for Guinness based in a small town in the Cotswolds with a BMW for a company car and earning two hundred grand a year, this is where you figure that out. We're going to worry about what might actually work later on.]

Now, where were we before we so rudely interrupted ourselves? Ah yes, your thoughts on all the above, please?

_____

_____

_____

_____

_____

9. Your finances

Hmm. Starting your own business is certainly going to have some effect on your finances. And that will almost certainly be a negative one at first, and it may even continue that way as time goes by – the pay-off being the lifestyle options. Here are some things to think about:

- **How important is money to you?** How much do you actually need/want, and how much do you think you need/want? What about in a few years time? If you've got four kids and plan to put them through independent schools, this may not be the best time to go into something risky.

- Most businesses have set up costs, though not always. **How much cash do you have available right now to sink into your business?** If the answer is about ten quid and you want to buy an ice-cream franchise, you may have a problem. There are ways around this of course – buying equipment slowly as the work comes in, keeping your job or going part time until you have enough private work to fund you, that kind of thing – so don't rule out your dream job (yet) just because you don't have the money.

- Sometimes it works the other way and your business will make you scads of cash. Woo hoo – excellent! That's obviously what you want to aim for, and soon we'll get into ways to make sure it happens. Just bear in mind that it may take you a bit longer to get to that point.

- Ultimately, though, think about your dreams. If what you really want is a job you love that earns you enough to pay the mortgage and go on a trip once a year, that's great. If your dream is to be hugely rich and able to fund your extended family's mortgages, that's wonderful. Figure out what you would like in the finances department, and in the rest of the book we'll help you get it.

So, what do you think?

_____

_____

_____

_____

10. Your qualifications

If you've got some and they're the right ones, that's great! If not, do you need them? This will depend on the field you're going into, its regulatory requirements, marketing issues and your experience and confidence level.

- *Regulatory requirements.* If you want to set up as a **freelance architect**, for example, you're obviously going to need the right qualifications – a degree from a registered institution and membership of the professional body, not forgetting about liability insurance (sometimes that's a compulsory part of being a member of the professional body). If you want to be a **practitioner of architectural services**, however, offering interior design yourself and perhaps subcontracting in an architect, you might want an interior design degree or diploma instead. It might be different again if you are happy to call yourself an **interior decorator**, rather than an interior designer. If you want to be a **gardener**, a qualification in horticulture may be a good marketing tool, but realistically it's not necessary. And so on, through the different areas. Sometimes it may be a simple change in terminology that decides whether you need to go back to university for years. Ensure you do your own ultra-thorough research in your special area – don't go on what your mate Barry told you his cousin did. If one exists, ring the professional body and clarify what qualifications you need. If there isn't a professional body, the odds are you don't need qualifications. Talk to people in your chosen industry. Google it.

- *Marketing issues.* Sometimes people want to know that you've got the qualification. More often, they don't. This may surprise you, but a lot of the time if you set yourself up as a specialist in widgadgetry, people accept what you say and don't think to check what makes you an expert. (That's why consultants who start by talking about themselves and their qualifications are doing it all wrong, by the way – they need to be listening, not describing where they went to university.) More of that in the marketing chapter but, meanwhile, if you think you need the qualification just for the sake of impressing people (not for the knowledge it brings or statutory requirements), think again. Your experience and charm may well be enough to carry you through. Quite often, too, to be *studying* the qualification actually has the same degree of impress-effect as having *completed* it. So consider starting, being able to say 'Yes, I'm doing my Master's in Marketing', but take it slowly. Don't feel you have to rush to the finish line to get the letters after your name.

By the way:
- **Don't** try to do something you don't have the qualifications or experience to do. Bad idea, it will end in tears, really it will.
- **Don't** stretch the truth. Ditto.

- **Do** get in touch with the relevant professional association, where applicable, for up-to-the-minute advice. Bear in mind though that some organisations may encourage you to become a member when it is possible, or even preferable, to ply your trade without such an affiliation.

Another thing to think about here is whether you simply want to do more study, just for the sake of it. That's hugely valid too.

So what about you and your qualifications? What have you got, and what might you need? What do you not need, but fancy acquiring anyway?

_____

_____

_____

_____

_____

11. Your status

Some people really don't care about status, and good on them. If you're one of them, move on now.

For the rest of you still here, we'll tell you a secret. One of the authors of this book doesn't give a rat's. But the other one really quite cares about status. Embarrassing as it is to admit, there's something about swanking around telling people impressive stuff that rather appeals. 'I'm just working on my latest book...the publisher in London expects this one to do even better than the last one...' – that kind of thing. Getting out the Blackberry® in the middle of every conversation...

OK, back to you. If you have a suity job in the city but your dream in terms of lifestyle is to be a gardener, if it's going to bother you to tell people you're a gardener, have a good hard think about this.

Does you it bother you so much that it would impede you being happy in your new life? Could you tell people you're a small business owner, or would you just lie and say you're a British Airways pilot and move on? Will it bother you at dinner parties? Do you actually secretly like hopping into your suit and doing the commute and having everyone looking at you, being impressed that you're, you know, in a suit?

For a lot of people this is tied up with material things – gadgets like the latest mobiles and cars. For others it really is about what's on the business card.

How much of an issue is this for you? Truly.

_____

_____

_____

_____

_____

12. Location

- Some jobs are only available in big cities.
- Some jobs are available in limited quantities in regional centres.
- Some jobs can be done by using email and occasional travel while working from home/a small town. Some can't.
- Some jobs can only be done from small towns or country areas.

Again this comes back to personal preference. Don't assume that you won't be able to do your dream job in a certain area, such as a small town. Start with your dream, then think about doing your research. Is the market in the small town bigger than you think? Can you spend time in a bigger city nearby and tap into that market? Can you live in a small place and commute weekly into the big city?

(Eventually, when we stop dreaming and start being practical, you'll need to remember your family here too. If you have a partner, you'll need to factor in his or her job choices; and schooling/childcare options if you've got kids. But let's not go there right now.)

So, dreaming. Where would you _love_ to live? If it's where you _do_ live, congratulations. It's a strange thing when you think about it, but lots of people live in places they aren't particularly thrilled about, just because it's where they grew up or where their family lives or some such.

But even though we're talking dreams here, that doesn't mean they shouldn't be based in reality. If you've nominated somewhere to set up shop, do see if it's even vaguely viable before you build your whole life around that plan. Spend some time there if you can. Get the local paper, talk to people, become familiar with the area and the players. Picture yourself living and working there. Figure out if it's a pipe dream or an actual real-life, I-want-to-do-it-dream.

If your dream is to have a city pad *and* a country getaway, that's fine – that goes in this section too!

_____

_____

_____

_____

_____

Analyse this!

If you really enjoyed this whole form bit, go back and do it again. And there are lots of formal and informal places that do this kind of thing in more depth than we have room for, so if it *really* rings your chimes, consider putting some time into:

• Careers counselling

Meeting one-on-one with a career counsellor or adviser to talk about you, you, *you*! See www.counselling-directory.org.uk/career.html or ask around for a referral.

• Personality testing

Myers-Briggs, DICE, Enneagram…there's a whole stack of measures of personality. See www.myersbriggs.org or other authoritative personality tests.

• Job suitability analysis

You can do things such as John Holland's Self Directed Search, where you fill out boxes and it tells you what kind of person you are and what sort of jobs might suit. See www.self-directed-search.com.

We don't necessarily recommend one of these measures over another. Start with a Google search and then figure out what you like the smell of.

Putting it all together

So now you've got a dozen different thoughts and ideas about what you might want from the next phase of your life.

You know what? Lots of people never get this thoughtful *ever*. In fact, you may not have done so yourself up until this moment.

And now you know what shape you'd love your life to take – in dreamland. The next step is to turn those dreams into, well, your actual life.

First, you need to get even more selective and work on priorities. You may have to decide between dreams. (Don't come to us looking for sympathy: if that is how you end up, at least you're loose in the sweet shop, with a basket that won't hold everything.)

Now go and get a highlighter pen, if you don't mind, and go back through your answers again, reading over what you wrote above and putting in answers below.

First. Which *one* of these dreams is *most* important to you?

_____

_____

Next. Which ones will you be really, really disappointed about, if you get to your 80th birthday party and haven't achieved them?

_____

_____

And finally. Have you actually already achieved some of these childhood dreams?

(If you have, it should make you feel good to know that.)

_____

_____

Now tear out this page and stick it to your wall. And look at it for a couple of days.

The more you know about yourself and your innermost wishes, the easier it will be for us to help you get there.

Next – learn how to make it happen. Keep reading, it's about to get really interesting.

CHAPTER THREE

QUESTIONNAIRE: REGRET AND HAPPINESS

For anyone thinking about starting their own business...the most successful business owners are hard working, open minded, prepared to listen to others and like to have fun! Alison Richardson, Richardson Associates

Never think starting a business is going to solve any of your problems. If you're not really up to it, don't even start. Don't guess, be sure. If not, it will only add to the problems you already had. Frank Willems, At Ease BV

Apparently the life motto of well-known, burly Australian billionaire James (son of Kerry) Packer is 'he who dies with the most toys wins'. This is pretty sad when you think about it. In the long run we're all dead, and the amount of stuff accumulated at the point of snuffing it is not likely to be much consolation, one wouldn't have thought – not least because this billionarie's personal wealth more than halved (as did most people's) during that stomach-churning economic rollercoaster ride at the end of 2008.[4] Somehow 'he who dies with less than half as many toys as he had six months ago' doesn't carry quite such an impressive swagger, does it?

As has been pointed out (anonymously, unfortunately – we'd love to shake his or her hand) no one's last words – presumably not even those of a billionaire – are likely to be 'I wish I'd spent more time at the office'. Far, far too many apparently rich and successful businessmen and yes, businesswomen too, barely ever see their children while they are growing up, and by the time they realise, it's too late to do anything about it.

On the other hand, there are undoubtedly talented and intelligent people

---

[4] www.news.com.au/couriermail/story/0,23739,24585873-5007191,00.html

who spend a life in drudgery and hopelessness, whose last words might be something like 'I could have been someone'. And that's pretty awful too. Ambition is good – very good – when taken in balance with all the other things you care about.

It's time to take a good hard look in the mirror. Do you see someone who's made a stack of cash and is loving life? Or perhaps you see someone who's made a stack of cash and, quite frankly, doesn't feel that sense of fulfilment and happiness they'd hoped for? Leaving the cash to one side for a moment (keep it where you can still see it out of the corner of your eye if you're happier), consider this question instead: 'What matters – what *really* matters – to me? What are my values?'

And having worked out an answer to this (you haven't done it yet, have you? Don't worry, we're all going to do it together in a minute), the next step is to measure how you actually behave alongside those values. In other words, if you feel that family, say, is very important to you but you're spending 14 hours a day working, then perhaps there's a discrepancy. 'Ah, but I'm providing for my family,' you may say, and of course you are – and we like material things too, not least food, clothes and housing, as well as holidays, iPods and plasma TVs. However, whether your family might prefer to see you occasionally is another issue altogether. (They may not, of course – you may be such a terrible pain in the arse, the less they see of you the happier they are. But you see the relevance of the question.)

So here's another questionnaire. (You should be getting used to them by now. They're good for the soul, honestly.) A couple of observations about this. You may find it confronting. So you should: if you don't, you're not doing it right. And you should take care to ensure your answers are confidential. This not so much for the protection of others who may be surprised by your answers, though that's true, as to ensure that you are absolutely up front and say what you really mean. That's important.

Part A: You and your life

What are your most important values in life? Below are some ideas to get you started. Try hitting the ones you like a *lot* out of that long list with a highlighter pen. When you've done that, go through it again and imagine you can only have *five* (for you personally). That means leaving out many, many values that you'll surely find difficult to live without. Still, which five do you choose?

What do you value?

accomplishment/success	country, love of	global view
accountability	(patriotism)	good will
accuracy	creativity	goodness
achievement	customer satisfaction	gratitude
activity	decisiveness	hard work
adventure	delight of being/joy	harmony
all for one and one for all	democracy	helping others
ambition	discipline	honesty
arts and culture	discovery	honour
authority	ease of use	humanity
beauty	education	independence
calm/quietude/peace	efficiency	innovation
care	environment	integrity
challenge	equality	intellect
change	excellence	intelligence
cleanliness, orderliness	fairness	justice
collaboration	faith	knowledge
commitment	fame	leadership
communication	family	looking after yourself
community	family feeling	loyalty
competence	flair	love
competition	fitness	manners
concern for others	freedom	maximum utilisation
content over form	friends	(of time/resources)
continuous improvement	friendship	meaning
cooperation	fun	mental health
coordination	generation	merit

modesty	resourcefulness	stability
money	religion	standardisation
openness	reputation	status
others' view of you	respect for others	strength
peace/non-violence	responsiveness	succeed (a will to)
perfection (e.g. of details)	results	success/achievement
personal growth	romance	support
physical health	rule of law	systemisation
pleasure	safety	teamwork
politics/political party	satisfying others	time awareness
positive attitude	security	timeliness
power	selflessness	tolerance
practicality	self-reliance	tradition
preservation	self-respect	tranquility
privacy	service (to others/society)	trust
problem solving	simplicity	truth
progress	skill	unity
prosperity/wealth	socialising	variety
punctuality	speed	wisdom
quality of work	spirit in life (using)	your self view
regularity in your life	sports	

What about for other people? What do you admire in others? What are the values you'd like to instil in your children, should you be blessed with any little goslings to cherish?

_____

_____

_____

Rank the following in order of importance to you, from 10 (highest) to 1 (lowest):

accomplishment	love	prosperity
challenge	patriotism	status
family	prestige	success
honour		

Now take a minute to consider how you live your life, and rank those same words as you feel your life exemplifies them, from 10 (highest) to 1 (lowest):

accomplishment	love	prosperity
challenge	patriotism	status
family	prestige	success
honour		

Transfer your two different rankings to this table:

	Importance	How I live my life
1		
2		
3		
4		
5		
6		
7		

8		
9		
10		

Note the three most significant differences between what you value and what you do. If you don't find any distinctions, then you're either highly unusual and admirable, or perhaps just a little self-deceived. If you're the latter, you'll assume you're the former and will give yourself too easy a time. If you're the former, you'll assume you're the latter and give yourself too hard a time. Now you just have to decide which of these you are!

What do you notice? And how do you feel about these discrepancies?

_____

_____

_____

If you had to choose (and you do), which **one** of these do you want more of?

happiness	money	sex
love	respect	time

Why?

_____

_____

_____

And if you had to throw one overboard – i.e. you could have more of all of them except one – which would it be?

happiness	money	sex
love	respect	time

Why?

_____
_____
_____

What has been the happiest **moment** of your life so far?

_____
_____
_____

What has been the happiest **month** of your life so far?

_____
_____
_____

If you ever worry (and who doesn't), which of the following are you most likely to worry about?

• money and what it can bring
• safety, health and security of your loved ones
• work issues
• your health
• your relationship with loved ones
• the state of the world today

Are your worries realistic or are they, you know, worries?

Part B: Your working life now

Describe your working life in three words.

_____

What's the best thing about your work at the moment?

_____

What's the worst?

_____

CASE STUDY

Interview: Malcolm Parr, bookkeeper

Malcolm has started up businesses twice; a printing business and a multilingual brochure business. He is now a bookkeeper.

'I left school at 16, despite doing well there – I'd just had enough. I came from a family of printers and decided that was what I wanted to do (to their disappointment). So I became an apprentice at the London College of Printing, and also took an ONC (Ordinary National Certificate) and an HND (Higher National Diploma) in Printing Technology.

'When I finished my apprenticeship at about 22, I thought I should stay with the same business that had supported me and give something back. Then at about 24 or so, I moved into the office.

'In 1986 I realised that myself and two others had a good mix of skills between us to start up a business: we had the sales skills, the technical knowhow and the production expertise. We bought a £500k printing press and away we went.

'Things went really well for about 17 years...and then we went bust! Our bank decided that it was no longer happy with us having a big overdraft and wanted us to factor, which just didn't work for us. And to be honest I think we got a little complacent and maybe even arrogant.

'From there, we then decided to get into a language translation business. We'd had a department before that printed multilingual brochures, so it wasn't quite the odd move it looks.

'I was the youngest of the three directors. The other two were at a different stage in their lives and we just realised that it wasn't going to work this time round. So we carefully planned a wind-down of the business, which suited us all.

'That left me, in December 2005, aware that I was to all intents and purposes unemployable, in the sense that I really, really didn't want to work for anyone else. Actually I did try it briefly – for six weeks! It didn't work out. Our styles were so different and I found I just couldn't work the way this guy wanted. So that really did confirm my belief that the way for me was not to work for others.

'I considered a few different things – a jewellery store was one. Fortunately I had a friend in that business who helped me look at my plan objectively, and he didn't believe the premises were right. It was very valuable to have someone who could talk me out of a wrong move. I also bought an Internet advertising franchise, but that really didn't work out. It involved too many small transactions which just didn't build anything.

'Then I realised that in the two businesses I'd run, I'd been the one looking after the finances. So I thought that bookkeeping was the way to go – and that's what I did. I spent three or four months training with the Institute of Certified Bookkeepers, with the training run by Sage. It didn't actually take all that long, but I spent a fair bit of time waiting for assessments and marking to be done and so on.

'Now I have about three days' work a week, with more clients about to come on board. It's a low-risk venture that's scaleable; it gives me flexibility and freedom, and I'm based at home. Plus, of course, I'm not working for anyone else!

'For me the big lesson, right the way through, is that having 20 years' experience of business is great, but you won't have any problems to solve unless you can win the business in the first place. When the three of us started up, the one thing we didn't have was business nous – but we thought (and we were proved right) that you can learn that. What there's no substitute for is getting the business. So for me the really crucial question is this: how are you going to get your sales?

'The other big lesson, which isn't for when you start out but when you really begin to succeed, is to make sure that you keep your feet firmly on the ground. It's so easy to start thinking that you've done the hard yards and now it's time to reap the rewards. What can happen then is that you take your eye off the ball, at the same time as you're building up the overheads. And if you've got low overheads to start with, just a couple of big cars and bigger salaries can make a disproportionate difference. It can all really slip away from you so fast.

'For example I'm working with a business now which is just into its fourth year. And I can see the signs. One of the guys has taken his eye off the ball because he's building a house, and suddenly they're all wondering what's happened to their cash flow. It's so obvious from the outside. So you've got to keep that level of desire just as high as when you started.'

Part C: Your ideal working life

Describe in three words how you would *like* your working life to be.

_____

What would be the best thing about it?

_____

What would be the worst thing about it?

_____

Part D: Cutting the cord

What is your timeline? How soon do you wish (intend) to realise your goal of working the way you want?

_____

Why is this your timeline?

_____

_____

_____

Why *wouldn't* this work for you? What are the three major obstacles that prevent you from plunging in?

_____

_____

_____

_____

_____

Know thyself

Finally, it's time to tie all these answers together. We hope you've found them stimulating and challenging, perhaps even a little scary. They are designed to bring to the surface things we often keep buried deep within ourselves, that many of us actually go through our entire lives without confronting. Just thinking about them already puts you ahead of the pack, which is a good place to be.

It's important that you don't look at your answers for a couple of days, perhaps even a week or so. Let them go cold on you and then revisit them. If you've forced yourself to be really honest, you are likely to be experiencing a combination of emotions: irritation (because you knew many of these answers all along and have learned nothing); frustration (because they have highlighted things that you currently don't believe you can do anything about); and perhaps anger – either at us (because we wrote the questions) or at yourself (because you spent so much time doing these bloody stupid questions and it's all just a load of psycho-babble anyway).

You'll notice these are what you'd traditionally call negative emotions. We're supposed to keep things like irritation, frustration and anger buried, not stimulate them. But that's OK, because the first step on this journey you're taking is to do exactly what you're not normally meant to – to stir up the mud at the bottom of your personal pool.

We'd like you to consider that if you already knew some of the answers, at least you now have the satisfaction of having confirmed them; that the frustration you feel at things you don't believe you can change is really pent-up energy that can be used to make those very things happen, and that any anger you feel at the questions, at us or at yourself is likely to be anger that your life isn't where you want it to be. After all, we invited you to answer the questions and you accepted the invitation. Now why would you do that, we wonder?

CHAPTER FOUR

BUILDING YOUR GOALS

> Go out and do it, even if it's just for the sense of adventure. Great things will happen if you apply discipline and hard work, no matter what the task is. Andy Roy, FInstIB, NeXus Management Solutions

It seems that it's important to humans to have something to aim for. It's not the arriving: it's the driving.

Of course, having life goals is not *essential*. That much is obvious, since the great majority of people who have ever lived have been too concerned about not getting killed to worry about what it's all about – but it does appear to make a big difference to those who have the luxury of fretting about these issues.

Here's a real-life example. A client of ours, let's call him Mark, was a successful, well-adjusted, prosperous businessman. In his mid-50s, he had achieved pretty much everything he'd ever set out to do. It sounds idyllic, doesn't it? The fact was, however, that his business was stalling and his life was stale. He was struggling and unhappy, and what made it worse was that he didn't know why. It is pretty dismaying when you have money, a wife who loves you, kids working in the business, success…and a general feeling of malaise.

So, what was Mark's problem? It was this: he'd achieved everything he'd set out to do, and now he had nowhere to go because he hadn't prepared himself for what he was going to do when he'd got where he was going.

(The rest of the story isn't really relevant, but perhaps we shouldn't leave right there. What happened to Mark? Easy, really: we worked with him to come up with a new business destination, and before you knew it the business was flying again and the buzz was evident all round the place.)

The point of all this isn't Mark and his business. It's this: what drives you is where you're headed. Set yourself a destination and you'll work towards it. Actually, it doesn't even feel this way, as we know from experience. It's more that if you set yourself a destination, *it* will pull you towards it. No longer do you have to find the energy to drive yourself on; where you're headed will do most of the dragging. If this sounds a little unlikely, believe us – it works. Here's how.

Pull up a chair, sit yourself down and take out the notes you made in the last bit. All that stuff on hopes, dreams and where you really want your life to be going.

What does it tell you? Write the answer here:

_____

_____

_____

_____

_____

Now, bearing all that in mind, let's turn it into something real. What about success? You want a bit of success...don't we all. And you want *your* success, not anyone else's. So have a think and decide exactly what success means to you.

What is success? Write the answer here:

_____

_____

_____

Now take those ideas of success and be as absolutely specific as you can. For example, did you write 'money'? OK, let's go with money – money, money, money. (Actually it almost certainly isn't money: very few people want money, they want what money can buy. But it'll do for the time being.) So, how *much* money? A million? Is that enough? It sounds a lot, but is it really? Or 100 million? Why? What difference will 100 million make that 75 or 90 or 97.5 million won't? Why aim for more than you really need?

Did you write 'time with family'? Or 'a successful business'? Or 'a holiday house'? Whatever it was, quantify it – figure out what it means and how much you want. That gives you your target.

What do you need? What's your target? Write your answer here:

_____

_____

_____

So let's say, for the sake of argument, that the goal is money and 20 million is the amount, because what we need to do can't be done on less and doesn't need more. Imagine now you have your 20 million. Two questions.

First question: how do you know you have 20 million? Silly question? Go with us for a moment here. Be literal (and that's the point): how, *precisely,* do you know you have 20 million? Is it, for example, the bank statement? Is it, maybe, the sight of ginormous numbers of banknotes piled up in, er, piles on your coffee table? OK, whatever. But if you don't know how you know that you know what you know, you won't know that you know what you know. (This sentence is a tribute to Donald Rumsfeld – remember him?)

Second question: how does it feel? Yes, fantastic, wonderful and all that. But literally, specifically and in minute detail, how does it feel? How does it look to you? What does success sound like for you?

Try that for a minute. You'll notice two things. It's not easy (because you ain't never had 20 million, so you're imagining something outside your experience); and at the same time, surprisingly, it's easy too. You *know* what it feels like to make money, to do well, to be successful.

So what you need to do is to capture that feeling, in its absolute joy and absolute essence. Close your eyes for a moment and just savour that flavour. Let yourself know the feeling and become familiar with it. In doing so, notice where in your body you feel it. In your stomach? In your gut? Or maybe in your heart? Perhaps in your head? Wherever the feeling is, try and measure it out of 100...and then try and increase it by just a few per cent. What you're beginning to do is to isolate the feeling itself and to increase it. If it comes with pictures, see them as clearly as you possibly can – and then turn up the sharpness and brightness, increase the size and do whatever it takes to get that feeling, that image, as clear and intense as you possibly can.

(By the way, if you've done much management training you'll have a fair idea where the above and what follows come from. It's Neurolinguistic Programming (NLP), or a brief form thereof. It's not important that you know where it comes from, nor that you don't. But if you like the sound of it, look it up in Wikipedia and Google it: there's a lot of good stuff around about it.)

Now you have your ideal goal, it's time to use it. You know what success feels like, looks like, tastes like. Now, put a date on it. Don't say 'tomorrow', because this is going to take some work (we're coming to that). Equally, don't say 'ten years from now', because few of us can keep up our energy to work on something so far away, at least not without some intervening big goals that get us along the journey. Perhaps think in terms of two or three years from now. Make a date, a very specific one. Work out what day of the week it is (your PC time and date function can tell you that). Decide where you're going to be and what you're going to be doing when that time arrives. Set it all up in your head.

Next, write it down, in great detail. Start a document – PC or paper, it doesn't matter. (We like to do this on a computer so we can make the document password protected, so that it really and truly is ours and ours alone. For a more low-tech option, put it in an envelope in your sock drawer.) State what you're getting, what you're rewarding yourself with, how you know you've achieved what you've set out to achieve.

That's the reward. That's what you're working for. That's your deadline.

However, there's more to it than that. Anyone can write down what they want (though few do). The difference that makes the difference, however, is to work out what it's going to take to get there. You're going to have to work extraordinarily hard to get extraordinary results, and you shouldn't kid yourself otherwise. Every night when you go to bed you're going to need to be able to say to yourself, 'Today I did everything I could to achieve what I was after. I left no shots in the locker. I took no short cuts.' If, hand on heart, that's your true judgement on the day you've just completed, you can sleep the sleep of the just, knowing that it's not been wasted. Go like the clappers like that every day, in fact, and you'll hit your target ahead of time.

And it's more than just a vague commitment to work hard: you've got to work smart too. You've got to know what actions you need to take to get you along your path. Most of the rest of this book is taken up with suggestions, ideas and thoughts as to how you're going to do this. Again, write them down. Break down your success into chunks. What marketing are you going to need to have done to get to where you're headed? What sales? What do you need to have built?

Three years is a thousand days, approximately. There aren't many more than 250 working days in each year, which means you're down to 750. That means that a single week's work is a whole percentage point along your journey. So you don't really have any time to waste. Within 18 months you need to be more than halfway there, and you've got to allow for slippage, for difficulty, for delay.

Why? What does all this achieve? Our experience is that in fact a good, solid business plan (there's more on this elsewhere in this book), accompanied by a very clear vision of where you're headed, acts like a conveyor belt – or perhaps like one of those moving walkways at the airport. Suddenly you don't need to generate all the energy for yourself today, because you have the energy of your vision (or rather, the vision of its actualisation) to pull you towards it, and you have the detail of your business plan to light your way.

So, you've got your goal, and you know what values make you tick. Damned good start. What's next?

CASE STUDY

Interview: Raeleen Harper, Bowen therapist

Raeleen's interest in natural therapies took her away from a corporate marketing career to a Bowen therapy practice, which she is now combining with a growing clinical hypnotherapy practice. She is the Vice President of the Bowen Therapists Association of Victoria.

'I had a desire for greater independence, combined with a desire to study. I was going through a surgically-induced menopause, which was causing migraines I didn't want to take medication for. As a result I got referred to a Bowen therapist. [Bowen therapy is a gentle, powerful, non-invasive remedial technique which enables the body to restore its own natural homeostasis.] It worked so brilliantly for me that I had to learn more. So I studied anatomy and physiology for a year as part of a qualification as a remedial masseuse.'

Raeleen's studies have continued to the present day. Her practice is focused on women like herself, and her recognition that a large part of what they need is counselling led her to study clinical hypnotherapy, too.

'I started off working from home, but an unpleasant experience with a client speeded up what was a natural progression to a small clinic. (By the way, if you are working from home, I strongly recommend that you make it clear to your clients that you're not alone, even if you are.)'

Although Raeleen's business is not yet full time, she is getting busier and busier – and hasn't yet started up her advertising campaign, having got all her clients from referrals.

Lessons

1. Believe in yourself. (Raeleen recommends hypnotherapy to develop that belief!)
2. Give yourself permission to be successful.
3. Don't be afraid to ask for help – ask your peers, fellow students, teachers.
4. Just do it! Don't procrastinate, just get started and you'll be amazed.

Benefits

1. You'll discover a new level of self-esteem and confidence in your own abilities you may never have known you had.
2. Independence, not being answerable to anybody – it gives you time to research, explore and make things your own.

CHAPTER FIVE

WHAT SUITS?

I had a desire to have more control over my life. Alison Richardson, Richardson Associates

I had a few life-changing experiences – the straw was having worked for a pretty terrible business owner, and I figured if he could run a business then so could I! Luke Harvey-Palmer, Buzzle

Maybe you're reading this book because you know exactly where you're going, you just need a little help along the way. You know what it is you want to do – butcher, baker, candlestick maker – and you're just hoovering up whatever information you can get. Excellent. As we've said often enough, knowing where you're headed sure as hell beats not knowing. That's the good news.

The better news is that you probably actually don't even need to read this chapter and can flick straight on to the beginning of the next one. There, you've just saved 20 minutes of your life to do something else instead. As you whizz through, though, just pause every now and then and see whether there's anything that you find interesting. If not, terrific. Just give us just a minute and we'll catch up with you.

The rest of you are pretty clear about one thing: you want out. Either that or you don't have a lot of choice in the matter. Either way, you want to be working for yourselves – you're just not 100 per cent certain what job it is that you want to be doing when you work for yourselves. Fortunately you've come to the right place: that's the subject we want to cover very briefly in this chapter. With any luck, by the end of it you'll find yourself closer to knowing what your dream is.

Here, then, are a whole bunch of jobs that you could do if you were working for yourself. It goes without saying (actually it doesn't, or we wouldn't say it) that there are in fact many, many more variations on every-thing mentioned here – this list is just to get your juices flowing, to get you thinking in a creative way about solving the challenge of finding the thing that's really going to light up your life.

Let's have a look at this in more detail.

Work types

What are you interested in, exactly? Do you want to work with kids? Kites? Kittens?

Belinda, a friend of Steve's, was saying that she loves 'everything' about her current job. That struck Steve as odd. 'Including that psycho boss you're always ranting about?' he asked. 'Well, no, obviously,' she replied. 'What about the fact that there's no business currently, so in fact you're not getting to meet all those great creative people?' 'Shut your face,' she replied, wittily. And that was the end of that conversation.

But the point Steve was probably trying to make, in his own cackhanded way, was this: what *exactly* do you love? Do you love it all equally as much? Or are there bits of it you find splendidly marvellous and vice versa? Or are there some, to use the technical term, shit bits? In this chapter we'll be helping you sort out one from t'other.

Part 1: Work topics

Let's begin by examining and then throwing away one of your most closely-held assumptions: *that you're going to end up doing what you're qualified to do.*

At first glance, this seems pretty much like the best place to start. If you've spent years training to be a lawyer or an accountant, it seems pretty mad to ignore all that and, in effect, declare that you wasted all that time. However, this is *exactly* what we want you to do.

It may well be that, at the end of this process, you end up precisely where you started. Instead of regarding the exercise as a colossal waste of time, though, think of it as a testing procedure. If, on close and detailed examination, you discover that you do indeed want to do what you are already doing – but to do it for yourself – well that's a fine and great result. You can proceed safe in the knowledge that you're building on firm foundations. However, if you discover that you've 'wasted half your life', you have two ways to think about it:

1. 'I've wasted half my life. Bugger.'
   Or, alternatively:
2. 'I've wasted the first half of my life. Good job I found out, otherwise I'd wasted the second half too. Hurrah!'

Take a wild guess at which one we think is likely to be more productive!

So let's make a start with work topics. *What is your area of interest which you want to turn into a business?* For the time being, don't concern yourself with the format of your business, how you will structure it, how you can make it work...we'll get onto all that in a bit. For now, we're just looking at the area and the people and the stuff you want to work with.

The best way to think about this is not what work you think you can do, or what you are qualified to do, or even what you want to do, but instead to turn it round and think about *what you actually love to do with your time*. Just imagine how it would be if you could work with things you're interested in and want to spend your time doing. Wow!

Just for the moment, resist the temptation to throw your hands up (never a good idea when you're reading a book anyway) and exclaim that 'It can't possibly work'. There'll be plenty of time for that later: let the difficulties argue for themselves (as Churchill is by now getting pretty tired of repeating). For now, let's dream a little dream...

As you work your way through this, make a note every time you find something of interest. Hopefully by the end you'll have half a dozen possible areas you'd be happy spending your working hours doing. What you're looking for is things that get you going a little. Until this moment you may well have regarded them as evening or weekend things, things you couldn't possibly do during the daytime as well. Cast that thought aside and let's pretend, shall we?

1. Your current work. Or past work. Or something linked to it. Or something

This is the most obvious work area to consider and thus should be quite easy. It feels like this: you *know* this business, you have the contacts, your reputation precedes you, you know where the market gaps are. Etc.

The problem, of course, is that you may be so thoroughly sick and tired of the area you work in that you'd rather eat your own hair than set up your business in the same category. This problem needs to be faced up to. Let's do so then.

You are tired of what you do – mortally and, it seems, irreversibly tired of it. But think about it for a moment. Maybe the reason you want to set up on your own is to get maximum flexibility and lifestyle, or to get away from a particular boss you can't stand, or to make loads of money and retire to Spain. Maybe you actually *like* some things about your job – the topic, which you can take with you, for example. In that case, starting your business in your area of expertise is a stonking good option.

Steve kind of did this when he moved from the UK to Australia. He'd been in the magazine industry for ten years, and was pretty much bored to death of it. (The feeling, it must be said, was pretty well mutual.) However, when he migrated he found himself a job in…magazines. Why? Because although his ambition was to do something else eventually, he was trading in his experience to buy himself the opportunity to migrate. A price well worth paying, he now says.

Now, admittedly Steve wasn't moving into working for himself (at that stage), but you can see the point: sometimes life is a trade-off.

What options do you have, similar to your current work, that would allow you to work for yourself? Write your answer here.

_____

_____

_____

_____

_____

2. Sports, hobbies, interests

So that's fishing, golf, windsurfing, indoor rock climbing, chess, embroidery, motorbikes, photography, pornography, fashion, goats (or maybe the last four combined)…whatever it is that you like doing in your own time. Wouldn't you love to get paid for hanging about doing that kind of stuff?

Think about all the links in the supply chain for your interest – in other words, what happens between the product being created and someone (like you) getting into the activity? After all, *someone* has to:

- **plan and commission it**
- **design it**
- **make it**
- **wholesale it**
- **promote it**
- **get it in front of the public – retail it**
- **and maybe even teach it**

For example, say golf is your thing. You could be the person designing the golf clubs (though unless you're already an industrial designer or an engineer, that might take quite a bit of re-training); you might promote events at the golf club; you might run a golf shop or give golf lessons, or start an online business selling golf gear.

Then there are a whole bunch of other businesses that work around your core interest, rather than being directly involved. So you might organise golf tours of Spain, or create handmade leather golf bags, or take photographs of golf courses to sell within the tourism industry, or whatever else your imagination and skills can come up with.

Or suppose you're a musician, but there are no vacancies for Rock God and frankly you don't look quite as good in skintight leather trousers as you did. Who do you think owns all the independent musical instrument and CD shops? That's right – musician. It's a way for them to live in the world of music, while enjoying the benefit of two – heavens, sometimes even *three* – square meals a day.

The good thing about this is you probably know this stuff really well already, reducing your research. You *know* who is into the hobby, what kit they buy, where they go to buy it and do it, where they stay, the whole bit.

Is there a world in which you love spending time – or at least more time than you are spending now? Write your answer here.

_____

_____

_____

Here are some specific interests other people have built jobs around:

• Kids

Lots of people have them and there are a ton of businesses developed by people who have them/like them/want to work part time while bringing them up. These include:

○ starting up as a nanny or child minder at home or opening your own nursery;

○ opening an indoor play centre/soft play area with café;

○ retraining as a teacher;

○ producing stuff for kids – clothing, gifts, toys, educational stuff all seem to sell well online as well as in shops…and don't forget party planning;

○ becoming a specialist teacher/tutor in private practice – piano, tennis, literacy, maths and so on.

• Houses and gardens

Again, lots of people have them, and some people are really interested in them! Think about:

○ gardening – a bit of equipment and you can be out there trimming bushes and mowing lawns instead of being stuck inside your office. There are lots of specialist options here too: planting, cutting down trees, working with specific types of plants, focusing on homes or offices (looking after indoor plants in office buildings lets you smirk at all the people still stuck behind desks too);

○ interiors – interior design, cleaning;

○ real estate – buying or selling it; dressing houses for sale;

○ moving house – packing, relocating, moving things.

• Making/fixing things

If you've got the right kind of hands, this can be a really fun way to make a living. Think about:

○ becoming Mr/Ms Fixit – either for general or specialist stuff, like repairing vases, mobile phones, furniture, clocks;

○ being an artist or craft worker – perhaps you could make gorgeous handmade kits, stationery, t-shirts, pottery, glassware. It's hard to make a decent living at the more arty end, but don't forget selling your work at markets or online.

• Personal services

There is a huge area of activity around looking after people. Personal trainers, dieticians, naturopaths, beauticians, personal buyers, drivers, car washers – all these are having a big boom as people get more time-poor and asset-rich. As always, think about what you enjoy and see how you can apply that to a working career. If you're not into fitness and getting up early, personal training is not the right area for you!

What kind of people like this sort of work? Caring and energetic people, really. Do you dream of working closely with your customers and helping them transform their lives? This might be for you.

• Professional/money

There are numerous roles going in this area, and many of those in it are consultants and freelancers. Because the stock in trade is money, this kind of work is probably going to lead you into a better financial position than some others. (We said 'probably'. Don't get too excited: the hard work is still up to you.) On the other hand, you're still in a suit and tie and probably working office hours (maybe plus some evenings), so if lifestyle is what you're looking for, this may not be quite right. Think about becoming:

○ a mortgage broker – visiting people or having them come to you and working with banks to organise loans. A lot of brokers seem to work independently within larger organisations/franchises;

○ a day trader – though you probably need some serious money to start with (or someone who trusts you a lot!);

○ a freelance accountant/solicitor/whatever job you currently do in an office for someone else. Break out and find your own clients!

● **Volunteer work**

Lots of us do volunteer work of one type or another – usually for a cause that's close to our hearts, otherwise what are we doing there? If you do something voluntary that you enjoy, think about adapting it for your working day.

○ Can you work in the sector that is of interest to you – helping people while earning your own living? Contracting your professional services to not-for-profits or internationally is an obvious angle here. Helping them with fundraising or memberships would be an example.

You can also use the work you do for not-for-profits to gain new skills and meet key contacts. People in any not-for-profit will always be pleased when you put your hand up for extra work, and in return you should check that it's OK for you to add the organisation to your CV or use it as a referee. So if you want to set up a company doing event management for children's parties, pop in to your kids' nursery and have a chat about helping out. If you are keen to set up in media and public relations, try becoming the media spokesperson for an interest group.

Anything here grab your attention? What might work for you? Write your answer here.

_____

_____

_____

_____

That's a breathless run-through on the topic of work that might suit you. Relax – you're not making a decision, just exploring your options! All you need to do right here is just to make a list – there's something about *writing things down* that really makes them begin to seem real. Try it and you'll see what we mean. And be inclusive at this stage. If something has any merit at all, chuck it in. There's no advantage in cutting your options down at this moment: there will be plenty of opportunity to do that later.

CASE STUDY

Interview: Dawn Mancer, freelance marketeer

Dawn started out with a degree in programming and information systems. Now she works freelance with a marketing and public relations group.

'After university I began an 11-year career working for small to medium IT start-ups. At first I worked as a technical person and later became a specialist in technical marketing and pre-sales support. When I left my job, I was working 14-hour days, travelling the world, driving a smart car and earning around £70K – and that's a few years ago too. Now I manage a couple of hours here and there, drive a banger and barely cross the tax threshold, but hey ho!

'I was made redundant when the company I worked for went into receivership. Looking back I was quite complacent and comfortable – I wouldn't have moved without a shove.

'Now I combine working for myself with looking after my young son.

'I love not having to be polite to people that I don't like, a huge bonus for someone growing as old and as crotchety as I am. I can work in my pyjamas, listening to the radio and not feeling guilty for playing Solitaire when inspiration escapes me.

'Of course I miss having a fat salary, a semblance of status, foreign travel and the company of people who have no interest in crayons and nursery rhymes.

'Working for yourself can be as unstructured as you like it to be, this is great for flexibility but you have to be quite motivated to keep a pipeline going – it takes hard work.

'What advice would I give to anyone thinking about it? Three main things:

1. **Network** – you will be surprised at how many people you know know people who need your skills.

2. **Start slow with the advertising.** A card in the local shop can bring in enough business to start with. Marketing doesn't need to be expensive if it's clever.

3. **Don't be frightened of doing your own books** if you are a sole trader. You need to note things as they happen – income, expenses, invoices etc. But a simple spreadsheet should see most businesses through their first year. Remember your National Insurance and that you'll need to put aside money for the tax man.

'Working for yourself can be lonely with no one to bounce decisions off or share the responsibility of bringing in revenue. You need to be thick-skinned and capable of listening to your own counsel. There's no one to provide you with a pat on the back in the form of a review, bonus or payrise.

'Would I go back into the corporate world? I would rather eat my own liver – but I can envisage a time when perhaps it might be easier for me to get a job than for my husband. And if the devil was nipping at our ankles I would get on and do it, albeit with bad grace.'

Part 2: Work environment

Environment is one thing you really want to get right. If you're an outdoorsy person, being stuck in an office all day every day is going to drive you round the twist, no matter how interesting or well paid the job.

So, in what kind of place do you love to spend time? It's a remarkably easy thing to overlook, especially if you haven't had the opportunity to vary your environment very much, and getting this right tells you an awful lot about what you really want to be doing.

If you've always been stuck in a work cubicle, you may not even notice it any more. Equally, if you work outside and just love it, you may be unaware of how important it is to you. Where do you like spending your time? Do you, for instance, like professional offices? Don't scoff, some people do, you know. Or would you rather be in the garden? Do you need your own space? Are you happy to work alone all day, or do you need the buzz of the watercooler and the chance to nip out to pick up a coffee?

When you have an answer to this question, consider what type of business this leads to. If you need a professional office and like peace and quiet then running a shop isn't going to be your bag, fairly obviously. And if you can't bear to be in the office but have to be outdoors, then being a freelance piano tuner is going to drive you mad pretty much immediately. OK, so you probably already know you don't want to be a shopkeeper or piano tuner. But the point is, you haven't yet defined what you *do* want to do, and if you consider your work environment, you're likely to discover some important clues as to what turns you on.

Working from a home base has an impact on the family. It is difficult to tell a 5-year-old that now is not the time for joining in to play something, just because I'm in the house. Likewise, making and receiving calls on business when a child, radio or vacuum is blaring in the background is not 'best practice'. Geoff Cutter, Melbourne Business Foundations

Tick the one of these four boxes that most closely approximates to your idea of heaven:

☐ In your office/at a desk

This is Susannah. 'I quite like working at a desk,' she says. (Actually, she means she loves it.) 'I like the sense of order of keeping it tidy…having my own mug…getting to chat to workmates while I make a cup of tea. Nerdy, I know. I am a happy slave to the computer!' Yep, that's her alright. Is it you, though?

☐ In other people's premises

This is Steve's idea of heaven, and perhaps it's yours. Whizzing about, breezing in for an hour or maybe a day, then moving on to the next thing. What's so great about that? 'I guess I love the novelty,' Steve says, 'the change of pace, the fact you're seeing different worlds all the time. Variety, that's the thing!'

☐ At home

This can be either heaven or hell, and sometimes both. Answer your emails, hang up the washing; make a business call, put on the laundry. It's fabulous for flexibility and the ten-second commute – you can have a couple of hours work done before the rest of the world gets moving, or you can bash out a few emails when there's nothing on TV (i.e. all the time). And that's the trouble…it's not so good for having personal time, unless you're really disciplined about shutting down the computer at 5 p.m.

We also have a theory that it's energy sapping to be on your own for too long. We always get revved up when we meet and chat about what's going on…just the act of getting together stimulates us and gets the blood flowing. Too much time in the home office and you can feel the dust beginning to settle on the shoulders. But that's us and this is about you. If it works for you, fantastic!

☐ Outdoors

Ah, the fresh air and sun…and rain and snow and whatever else the weather throws at you! You're a special breed alright, and while we might like the occasional stroll, you're someone who only really comes alive when you're out there getting among it.

And now tick one of these three boxes:

☐ *I love* working with people

People who need people, so the song goes, are the luckiest people in the world. Well that's as maybe, but are you in that category yourself? You're not necessarily the life and soul of the place, though you may be, but it's definitely the case that you thrive on company. You need chatter and activity and to know what's going on (or 'gossip', as people who don't feel the same way tend to call it).

☐ I'm comfortable working with people

Far from being a recluse, you like company as much as the next person. But it's not an absolute requirement, and you won't go completely bonkers if left to your own devices for an hour or two.

☐ I like to work by myself

How can anyone concentrate and get anything done with all that chat, chat, chat going on? It's not that you don't *like* people, it's just a matter of concentration and focus. A little bit of peace and quiet and you can get a ton of work done. Then as soon as the chat starts up, you might as well pack it in…

Fairly obviously, the box you ticked here tells you an awful lot about where you need to be to work. If you ticked the last box, then being right in the thick of things is not going to get the best out of you. Conversely, if you need to be where the action is, then trying to set up on your kitchen table and seeing no one but the postman all day is rapidly going to lose its charm.

Career progression

Let's just clarify something before we go on. You're probably used to thinking of your career in terms of – well – a career, especially if you're a recent arrival or current incumbent of Corporate World. At least career progression, where you start with a junior job and inch up the Corporate World ladder until your seat is near the front of the plane, will be a familiar ambition.

But it doesn't have to work like that, you know. If you step out of Corporate World, you really have the option to create the job you want – the job you love – without everything that you don't like. But the career ladder may look a bit different to what you're used to.

For a start, you are now the MD, CEO, GM, ED, TURD (we used to have a boss like that)…whatever acronym the big boss used to have, that's you now.

Next, you may well find if you ever decide to go back to Corporate World that your experience in Entrepreneur World may not be as appreciated as it should be.

This is going to depend on a number of factors – your industry, what you're doing, your level of success and so on. But almost certainly, a lot of people in Corporate World have no idea of what it takes to run a small business (well, do you, at this stage?) and limited respect for some of the things an entrepreneur does. So if you hop out of Corporate World and then decide to go back five years later, you may well return to a job at the same level of seniority as the one you left, while your contemporaries have forged on in your absence.

This may or may not bother you. And it may not ever happen, because an awful lot of people leave Corporate World and would rather chew off their own arms than return. Only you will know if this is potentially on the cards for you (and you might not know until you get there).

Something else to think about as you work through this book is that we're not necessarily talking forever here. We're looking at ideas to make your working life happier and more successful for you. That means it needs to fit around your actual life and circumstances. And being only human, these change. You're looking for what suits you right now and for the next few years, and maybe a bit longer after that if you like, and longer again if it continues to suit. You might be thrilled to settle in Entrepreneur World for the rest of your working life; or just for a few years. So while you're reading, just remember: it's for as long as it does the trick and no longer. You get to make the decisions here, and you have options.

CHAPTER SIX

CHOICES, CHOICES: YOUR OPTIONS AND HOW TO FIND THEM

> **Commit to it, be passionate. Start it whilst in a day job so that the grunt work is done whilst you are salaried. Outsource what you can. Remember, nothing happens till somebody sells something.**
> Ashley Fernandes, *Crossing Cultures*

By this point you've figured out what you're interested in and what type of environment you'd like to work in. If you haven't, you're not yet ready to advance into this next section. We suggest you go back over the first part again and work out why you're not yet clear about what interests you and the kind of environment in which you thrive. Plough on without clarifying those basics and you're very likely to end up doing what your previous experience suits you for, rather than following your passion.

So, assuming you're OK with all that, let's crack on. In this chapter we're going to put it all together…by breaking it all down. What sort of businesses are out there? Which ones fit your requirements? And, crucially, which of these works *best* for you?

If you're anything like us, at this point it's all just a little overwhelming because *every* option is still open to you – and that means just about every kind of business on the planet!

To help you clarify your thinking, we've separated the options into major chunks:

- consultancy and freelance
- natural therapy and allied health professions

- retail
- teaching and training
- trades and services
- web business
- party planning and direct sales
- any other business (ha!)

And then right at the end we offer you a load of ideas for things you can do straight away if you're currently strapped for cash.

Enjoy!

Consultancy and freelance
What is it, exactly?

This means working in your current profession, maybe doing the same or a similar job but in a different environment – picking up small or large projects on contract, working from their office, your office or your home. So...

If you're an IT dude who loves to surf, what about becoming a contract IT support person specialising in surf wholesale companies?

If you're a marketing manager, go freelance and get hired by a variety of companies. Work from home instead of being a desk slave!

If you're a financial bod or work in a bank, how about mortgage broking or financial advising?

If you've ticked off general management at some stage in your career, you can become a broad-based 'business coach' like Steve – it's a licence to print money really (joke).

> **I wish I was starting in a community that I had already been working in. It would have made starting a little easier with at least some established relationships.** Stan Sweeney, Guidepost Strategies

It ticks the boxes if:

- you're **technically trained**, such as being an engineer or designer. In fact, your technical skills may be just as important as whether you've got a body of experience or not;

- you're relatively well advanced in your career already (this applies particularly if you want to go into a more **managerial style** function) – enough to feel confident you know your business and the market inside out;

- you don't mind **working alone** and you're confident enough to pitch your personal skills one-on-one (remember it's you you're selling, not a product). You like working with people; you prefer listening to talking and you scrub up well.

What you need

It'll be important to have a fair lashing of professional experience or qualifications in the role you want to do. Your clients will look to you to be an expert and a specialist, so you'd better be pretty impressive when the meter starts running.

Contacts are immensely useful – it will be hard work if you don't know anyone who might hire you or recommend you, just to get started.

But you don't have to do it all on your own. There are many organisations that give you the opportunity to work with other consultants and advisers. Steve got himself accredited by the Institute for Independent Business (www.iib.ws), an international body for senior business executives from every walk of life. Best move he ever made, he says.

Upside

- You get to use your professional experience, stay in an industry you know and have a real excuse for keeping in touch with workmates.

- A lot of consultancies start with very little in the way of overheads. You can work from home and walk lightly in the world.

- Your risk is spread. If one job drops off, you can keep going on the other jobs on your books as more come in. You get plenty of variety, since you're working for different businesses all the time.

Downside

You're still doing the job you were doing before, albeit in different surroundings. Did you see yourself making a more dramatic switch than this?

Probable income level

Not bad, if you can find the work. Your hourly rate might feel damn fine, considering it's all coming to you. However, don't imagine you'll get paid work 100 per cent of the time – there's a lot of business development involved. The general rule of thumb is that your utilisation rate (how much of the time you're actually getting paid that delicious hourly rate) is likely to be around 50 per cent, at least in the early years. It's tempting to imagine that if your hourly rate is £150 and you're working about 2,000 hours a year, then… Well, it ain't necessarily so. As you build your reputation and network it may become more necessarily so, but don't make the mistake of thinking it'll be a walk in the park. It takes discipline, focus and a lot of hard work to make the really big bucks in consulting. We talk elsewhere about the personality types who thrive on this type of business. Just ask yourself: are you considering this because you have a passion for the work, or because you've used consultants and reckon it looks like a pretty soft gig?

How do you get started?

Try and kick off with a piece of project work, big or small, from a friend, contact in your network or your current workplace.

What does it cost to get going?

If you don't need special equipment, you can set up on the cheap…quality business cards, a laptop, a logo and a basic website are the starting points.

If you're an architect or graphic designer or someone who needs specialised computer software, even more reason to get a job to start you off.

Top tips

This is the thing we did and it worked for us: going into partnership. Being self-employed can be a lonely road, so if you can find a similar soul to bounce ideas off, you might have more fun.

Oh, and don't be embarrassed to pick up a part-time job as reliable income while you get up and running. If it's related to what you're doing, it should be senior enough that you can go public with it – 'I also teach one day a week at Sussex University'. If it's a junior job that you're doing just to pay the bills, best to make it in a field removed from your consultancy targets. You really don't want to be caught stuffing envelopes by someone who is considering you as a high-level strategic expert.

Where to from here?
www.ukconsultants.net
www.top-consultant.com
www.iib.ws

Natural therapy (and allied health professions)
What is it, exactly?
If you're violently opposed to even the idea of health improvement that doesn't come in a bottle or syringe, then this probably isn't for you. For a surprising and growing number of us, however, there's a great attraction in the idea of a business that enables you to pursue your personal passion and help people at the same time. Teaching's like that, except it's not usually one-to-one; so is business consulting, which typically *is* one-to-one (at least at the independent business end of the market), since you're dealing mostly with business owners and their funny ways. So too, of course, is being a doctor, but we're presuming you don't have a decade handy to go through the required training. So too is being a dentist, but that involves peering into people's gobs, so that's out for starters.

In the immortal words of Blue Peter, here's one we made earlier: Steve. He became a business adviser and, through that experience, first encountered NLP (Neurolinguistic Programming – ironically, the world's worst name for a really intriguing nest of ideas around the use of language). Through that he became intrigued with hypnotherapy, went off and studied for two years (while he maintained his business consulting practice), and now he happily combines the two, with a large dollop of counselling involved in both. Earlier in the book you'll have seen the interview with Bowen therapist Raeleen

Harper and later you'll find one with kinesiologist Karen Dickson, and they both have been on journeys similar to Steve's.

In this area we'd include (and not discriminate between) natural therapies and allied health professions such as **Bowen therapy, counselling, hypnotherapy, kinesiology, life coaching, massage therapy, reiki** and **personal training**. These are all areas where you need some training and a huge interest and drive to help people's health and wellbeing – mental as well as physical.

It ticks the boxes if:
- like Steve, you've found yourself fired up by an intellectual journey or amazed at the power of the therapy you yourself have experienced;

- you've made the discovery that you needn't put up a barrier between your work and your personal interests. As so many of our interviewees have said, following your passion is a great way to end up loving what you do and doing what you love.

What you need
These careers require passion, a fair degree of commitment to the cause and the ability to study, almost certainly while you're holding down a day job. Don't underestimate how tough this is: you get home from a hard day at work and face two or more hours of study, and you give up precious weekends to get down to your books. Just because you love doing it doesn't mean it looks endlessly appetising when the sun's shining and your friends want you to come out to play!

Upside
- You're pursuing your passion.

- Without wanting to get schmaltzy (because a lot of this stuff is just like every other job – damned hard work, far too much paperwork and faff and not nearly as much of the thing itself as you'd like) there is deep satisfaction in working with people to help them access their resources and make better choices. There is no satisfaction in Corporate World that comes close to seeing a client whose life has been transformed by work you've done with him or her.

Downside
- See the next few lines (we bet you could see this coming, couldn't you?).

Probable income level
While it is perfectly possible to make big bucks in this area, our experience suggests that you're not likely to. Steve, for example, takes a pay cut every time he sees a client for clinical hypnotherapy, rather than a business client (not that he's complaining – he's just *saying*).

How do you get started?
Almost without exception, the many people we've talked to in this area have developed an interest in the type of activity – 'modality', in the jargon – through personal exposure to it. Due to its great impact on their own lives, they've gone on to study it, prompted either by intellectual curiosity, desire to know how it works, desire to master its techniques so they can apply them for themselves or sheer passion to be practising what they've experienced. And that, of course, means they're driven by a hearty desire (the term is chosen carefully), rather than by any dull sense of duty.

What does it cost to get going?
It's not cheap, because for most of these activities you need to do some fairly hefty training. The cost can be thousands – hundreds at the very least – not to mention the significant time commitment. But, as always in this area, if you're investigating because you truly love it, you don't resent the time, nor indeed the cost of learning.

Top tips
You do need to be cautious, of course: much of this field is loosely regulated, if at all, and if you choose the wrong course you may find yourself considerably poorer and not sufficiently wiser. So keep your wits and your wallet close by and your pen firmly in your pocket until you've done your homework.

But with that caveat in mind, we also need to say that, in our experience, the vast majority of people attracted to this area have outstanding ethical standards and are exceptionally generous with their time and their knowledge.

Where to from here?

If this sounds like you, the first step is to look further into your particular area of interest. Talk to your practitioner, ask her how she got into it and where she trained. Take a look at sites like www.healthypages.co.uk.

At the very least, try moving towards the light and see what happens. Who knows where you might end up?

CASE STUDY

Interview: Christine Spencer, contractor

Christine's background is in the airline/logistics industry. In 2006 the logistics business for which she worked as a senior manager was bought out. Christine decided not to take the overseas move she was offered, but to do her own thing instead. Just as she was setting up, however, she was offered continuing employment that enabled her to establish her own business while retaining the security of a paid job.

'It was something I'd been thinking about for years and the takeover gave me the impetus to finally do it. One of the reasons for it was that whole glass ceiling thing. As a woman working in logistics, I was constantly coming up against barriers. I was doing the work but not getting the job titles.

'I had my plans [to go it alone] all in place – then the day I was due to talk to HR about my package, they offered me a contract! While it's been a blessing, because it's enabled me to set up by myself with security behind me, it's also been a curse, because it's meant that I haven't fully committed to what I'm doing. I suppose I've done 'slow motion', which has given me lots of time to feel my way and plan my course. This year my own work will certainly expand, and there'll come a time when I want to move over to that fully.

'So it didn't quite work out as I expected, and I think that's a really important thing to be prepared for.

'I decided to continue with what I was planning to do, even if only part time to begin with. Certainly my plan is to go over to it full time.

'What's suited me to work for myself? Well, I've always been someone who thinks outside the box, someone who can come up with solutions and ideas. And even while I was in the corporate world I was working more at a regional level, rather than within a team – so I was sort of working alone in a way even then.

'Certainly it was the desire to be in control of my own destiny.

'The big thing for me was knowing what the "it" was. I knew I had experience in service, sales and procurement, and felt I was good at working with people and as a leader – but how was I going to package it? Actually, if I'm honest, I'm still not quite clear about that!

'So I think one really big question you have to answer is the obvious one: what exactly are you selling?

'What lessons have I learned? Lots of things – eight, actually:

1. **Be clear about what you're doing.** I see so many people who bill themselves as "aviation experts" or experts in this or that, who really don't have any clarity about what they're doing with all that expertise.

2. **Research, research, research.** Get a really good handle on who and what's out there – what your competition is. If you don't know what you're up against, you won't be prepared.

3. **It's hard – much harder than you think – to communicate what's in your head.** Even when you are clear about what you're offering, somehow it's difficult to translate that into generic statements that mean something to people from different industries and experiences. So it's vital to start work on that early, and really get it right.

4. **There's lots of free advice out there!** That's great in one sense, because you'll need it yourself. But it also means that, if you're in the business of consultancy or advice, you have to make it clear that

what you're offering isn't the same as the information people can get from the FSB (Federation of Small Businesses) site, for example.

5. **Don't do the hard sell.** I'm active in BNI (Business Network International) and I use my slots not to sell, but to do ten-minute information and education sessions. So instead of saying 'Here's what I do, isn't that great', it's more about illustrating my capabilities. I suppose it's offering a taste, to see if they take the bait. Give something away for free and people will get a sense of what you do and how you work.

6. **Make what you do target-based.** With everything I do, my clients know exactly what they're going to get for their money. For example, I've been working with a personal trainer and each session we agree on a project or an activity that he'll undertake for the next week. I got an email from him just recently because he'd got six clients from just one of those activities! People need a reason, a result they can track from working with you. Otherwise they can come to believe that they'd have done all that stuff without you anyway. Your clients need to know when they're passing the road signs, as it were – otherwise, how do they know they're getting value for money? And it's also a kind of accountability. If they're not doing what you've agreed, they're not living up to their part of the contract.

7. **You have to be able to offer value, without the client losing face.** One of my clients was offering IP telephony and telling business owners they could save a ton of money if they used his services – which was tantamount to saying they'd made the wrong decision with their current supplier and should be ashamed of themselves! Instead it's a case of offering added value, of saying that we do what others do but we also offer much more. That's far less threatening. No one wants to be told they are stupid and have made a bad business decision.

8. **Improve your personal skills.** I'm a big advocate of NLP (neuro-linguistic programming). I think it has massive benefits for anyone in sales – and if you're running your own business, you will be in sales.

We've lost the art of conversation and NLP helps you learn it again. It means you can get a difficult message across without it coming out all wrong. You can say no nicely!

'What are the characteristics of people who work for themselves? Well, I'd use the word headstrong – untameable, in fact! We're people who don't fit the corporate mould. And often we find it hard to make a plan and then stick to it (and that's why I insist on targets for my clients). I guess that's because people running their own businesses often start up as a one-man band, with no background in the structured world of the corporates. I've been lucky to have that experience, which has helped immeasurably.

'And I have to say that some of my clients who run their own businesses are, in fact, unemployable. There's a self-assuredness about them that can even come across as arrogance. And there's sometimes a lack of people skills, which makes it difficult when they have employees and customers and suppliers!'

Retail

Just make sure you have a true passion for your business, as you are really tested and it's the passion that keeps you going. Richard Ferguson, Web Enhancer

What is it, exactly?

Fancy opening a golf shop, buying an embroidery shop or picking up a franchise for a pet accessory venture?

Running a shop doesn't just involve serving at the counter, you know. In addition, you'll be:

- **making or buying stock**
- **working damn long hours**
- **watching inventory**

- watching inventory shrink (jargon for getting stuff nicked, by staff or by customers. Calling it shrinkage doesn't lessen the pain one little bit)
- finding staff
- having staff
- losing staff and not having staff
- having good staff and worrying you might lose them
- having bad staff and worrying you might not lose them
- doing the books – not just bookkeeping and tax returns, but budgeting and crunching the numbers and working out how to increase the top half (revenue) and decrease the bottom half (costs)
- working damn long hours
- dealing with cranky customers
- not having any customers, cranky or otherwise, for what seems like weeks
- having too many customers, all in the shop as well as on the phone, and knowing that you can't deal with all of them and some of them are going to walk out and never, ever, ever come back in again
- marketing in a local community – frequent buyer programmes, advertising and so on
- working damn long hours

It ticks the boxes if:

You really do need to care about local community and like people. Seriously, most retail businesses are very reliant on passing trade and support from the neighbourhood. In a small retail business, you're going to want to focus on good service as well as good product – so chatting to people, putting up notices for school fetes and car boot sales, advertising in the local paper, that kind of thing. For most retail stores, the majority of traffic comes from within a mile or two.

The exception to this is if your business is so specialised that people drive for miles to come to you – if you're the only bookshop specialising in boating books in the South West, for example. In that case you're still working hard to be part of your local community, but it's the boating community. So you'll be advertising in boating magazines and tapping into boating networks and building a really good website, because a lot of your business will come from people who want to buy over the Internet rather than drive out to your shop.

You want to have a bit of a passion for your product if you can, and this is your chance to really immerse yourself in a world you love. A hint: if you're a golf fan and you know all about golf brands and equipment, don't open a scrapbooking shop. If you're a scrapbooking enthusiast and you're good on acid-free paper and die cuts and cardstock, a golf shop may not be the best choice for you.

What you need

Cash. Retail is not cheap to get into. As well as start up costs, you're going to want to have outgoings (rent, staffing, product, promotions) covered for at least three months, to give you time to get up and running and turning a profit.

Retail experience is always a good idea. If you've not got it, go and work in a shop for a few months – preferably in the same field as your proposed venture. At worst, you'll discover you hate, hate, hate it – and then you won't have to go through the trauma of starting something you don't enjoy. At best, you'll find you *love* it and get lots of tips on how things work (and areas you can improve), so you can launch your business fresh.

Upside
- Working with product you love – you get to choose what works, follow your hunches and try things out – and see if it works!

- If you do it right, your staff become like family.

- You can really tap into the local community.

- Get it right and the money comes in. When you sell, you can make some serious money – and kiss the shop goodbye for ever.

Downside
- Staffing – hiring, training, scheduling, managing. A lot of new businesses don't take on the admin load of staff at first, but you will need to, unless you want to work every single hour your shop is open and never go to the toilet.

- The grind. Monday, business is flat, another day at the shop and it goes on forever. It can be lonely and despite your best efforts you may well start hating your customers for being so stupid. And you can't go for a walk and buy a coffee to clear your head because your junior is off sick today… Seriously, if this sounds like absolute misery, then you won't be far wrong. Don't ever imagine that it's a walk in the park, retail.

Probable income level

Sorry, but it depends. Some retail businesses work right on the breadline or only survive because the owner has an independent income source or owns the premises outright (no rent).

Others are basically cash cows, with money walking in the door.

Yes, we know – you want to know how to tell which is which. Well, don't ask us because we don't know. If you buy a well-established business that's selling for a good reason (and you need to do your due diligence and work out why they're *really* selling), then you stand a reasonable chance – but of course you pay a premium for that comfort. If you reckon you can build up a dump and that's all you can afford, you had better be prepared for a long hard haul.

How do you get started?

There are three broad ways to get into a retail business:

1. Start from scratch

- You'll need to find premises – usually a shop for lease that's been doing something else; sketch out your business; buy in goods; hire staff; advertise; launch…the whole lot from scratch. This is the least expensive way of doing it – basically because you're doing the work of building up the business from nothing. So, no huge start up costs (other than renting your shop and buying stock and so on, of course).
- Because your business did not exist, your customers will have been buying from someone else or not buying at all. It will take a while for them to realise that being your customers is better than being someone else's customers. So don't get panicky if business starts with a trickle.

This is a good time to test out and make sure your set up is right, to get everything established, to do some promotion to get people through the door and start word of mouth. You'll need to make sure you're covered financially if there is a bit of a slow start. (And if your slow start is still slow after two, three, four months, you need to have a Plan B to address the situation quickly.)

- This is either a clever way of reaching a market no one else has noticed (What? There's no one selling pet accessories in your local high street? Ridiculous! Highest dog ownership per capita in the county!) or a really silly move, because everyone else has decided your high street just couldn't sustain a pet accessories business (and they may well be right). Oh dear, how to tell? (Don't worry, we do get into that later in the book.)

2. Buy an established business

- As suggested by Stuart Hayes of Starnext, it couldn't be easier: 'Buy an existing cash positive business and launch your ideas from within it.' You're buying a bunch of existing customers; stock range; possibly experienced staff, and hopefully knowledge and ideas about what works – excellent! For good or ill, you're buying an existing reputation. Of course, the trick is to keep the best and move on from the worst. A paint job and banner saying 'Under new management' may do the trick. Don't be in too much of a hurry to change things – take your time and find out first what your customers value before you rip everything to pieces.

3. Buy a franchise

- The UK franchise industry is vast – said to be worth some £10.8bn a year[5] – and you certainly pay for the privilege of buying an established brand. Think McDonald's and you're thinking about one of the world's most successful businesses, built on consistency and repeatability.
- Evaluating a franchise is way beyond the scope of this book and is a major task in itself. Get yourself as much information as you can about franchising, speak to as many experts as possible and be slow to whisk

---

[5] 2007 Natwest/bfa Survey

out the chequebook. There are franchises and franchises, and the differences aren't obvious. Talk to existing franchisees, and if the franchisor won't let you do this, draw your own conclusions.

What it costs to get going

Franchises are the most expensive option here, but then you're buying into a (hopefully) proven system and heaps of support.

At the bottom of the scale, renting out a local shop, having a painting party with your mates to get it looking decent and popping a few snappy looking products in the front window is a more accessible entry point if you don't have cash in the bank, or don't fancy a long, long, loooong chat with a bank manager.

Top tips

Location, location, location. If your shop is hard to find or difficult to get to or has no parking or is in an isolated spot, no one will come to you.

You may have wanted to open a funky gift shop for your entire life, but customers, fickle beasts that they are, don't care. Your gifts can be groovy and different and affordable and your marketing incredibly targeted and your staff friendly and service driven, but if people have to make a special trip to get to you, they won't.

We're sorry, but destination shopping really only works for Ikea and the like. For a start-up retail outlet, you *must* be somewhere where you get passing foot traffic and people can see you and find you easily. Honestly. Half the battle won, just like that. Oh, and decent parking or transport is a must. Sounds obvious and pretty dull, we know – but then that's retail all over: a game of inches.

Yes, we know the rent in prime locations is more expensive – far more expensive. But that's an illusion of course; it's more expensive to rent premises in the wrong location and have no one come to see you.

Where to from here?

There are many websites that specialise in buying and selling businesses and franchises, and magazines and brokers and agents too. We don't recommend any of these over any others – see what you like the look of and, of course, do your homework properly before you sign anything!

One absolute must is to get yourself along to a franchise exhibition – there's the Scottish Franchise Showcase at Glasgow Hall; the National Franchise Exhibition at the National Exhibition Centre, Birmingham; the Irish Franchise Exhibition at Dublin's RDS, and the Welsh Franchise and Business Show at Cardiff's magnificent Millennium Stadium.

www.businesslink.gov.uk includes solid information, as always, and is a good starting point.
www.thebfa.org
www.the-franchise-shop.com
www.whichfranchise.com
uk.businessesforsale.com

CASE STUDY

Interview: Michael Coleman, musical instrument retailer

Michael, his wife Roslynn and their three kids, Ryan, Tim and Amber, all work in Cranbourne Music, one of the most successful independent musical instrument shops in Australia.

Having started – but not completed – a business degree, Michael found himself very quickly in charge of a hundred staff in an ink company, squeezed between uncooperative workers and unsupportive management. 'I found it very frustrating having to out-think everyone, both up and down,' he says. 'Exhausting, actually. Eventually I quit, I couldn't see myself making money for someone else all my life.'

He sat down with his wife Roslynn and drew up a list of ways they could work together, which included retail options for both hardware, paint and music – an interest they both shared. 'We got lucky,' he says. 'It was almost as if the idea was waiting for us. As soon as we were open to it, like within a couple of weeks, there was a small ad in the paper for a shop in Cranbourne. I wasn't concerned that I didn't know the music business: I knew business – how to read a balance sheet and a budget, how to control overheads, how to get products in on time, stock turn (the number of times on average a product sells over a year) and so on. The business degree definitely came in handy!'

Lessons learned

1. Draw up a list and a two-year plan.
2. Follow your interest: you'll be much happier doing something you enjoy. You can go fishing with any kind of bait, but if you want to catch flathead there's a particular bait and a particular place you need to go.
3. Plan for things to happen and they'll come to you.
4. Start planning earlier. As Michael says, 'I wish I'd started planning a decade earlier for our exit from the business. We'd be further down the road by now.'

Teaching and training
What is it, exactly?

By teaching we don't mean wrangling with a bunch of stinky self-obsessed teenagers in a secondary school chemistry lab (Susannah is getting cold shivers just writing this). We're not going to talk about school teaching in detail because (a) it's not working for yourself, though it is a popular path for people wanting an out-of-business career, and (b) because it involves wrangling with a bunch of stinky self-obsessed teenagers in a secondary school chem lab.

The kind of teaching we have in mind is lecturing at university or instructing in a vocational college. It's often work you can pick up on a part-time basis and combine well with another new career; it sounds a bit impressive for other clients, and it draws well on your existing professional experience.

It ticks the boxes if:

- you enjoy **working with groups** or individuals – leading them, mentoring and introducing them to new ideas;

- you are **confident about getting up in front of a group**; if you're worried about public speaking, this probably isn't for you;

- your **detail-handling capability** is up to handling the marking and internal bureaucracy.

What you need

There are a whole host of new professional degrees springing up, often run by a small staff of overworked, stressed university employees backed by part-time industry professionals.

Here is where your industry experience is very well respected. Susannah and Steve teach marketing, communication and magazine editing at universities, despite neither of them having formal qualifications in these areas; and friends of Susannah's teach buying and fashion at a top vocational institution, after years in industry.

This probably won't work out if you worked in Corporate World for two years as a personal assistant, though; you probably want at least a decade of experience in a specific discipline under your belt at a reasonably senior level.

If you want to work full-time as a university lecturer, you probably need a PhD or at least be doing one. For part-time work tutoring or lecturing one or two days a week, in a professional programme, often your professional experience is what counts.

Upside

A day or two a week of regular work, getting you out of the office/house. What could be better?

Teaching at university or college is often very well respected by the public (read: your customers); it's regular, part-time work you can boast about.

Downside

Teaching is a whole new thing, so if you've not done it before or trained formally, there's a lot to learn. It's really important to find a buddy in the institution to guide you through both the teaching and the internal processes while you get started.

Pay! While the hourly rate for lecturing looks good, often the rates for tutoring and marking and so on aren't, and getting paid for a one-hour lecture means prep, getting there, doing the thing, getting back…for one hour of pay.

Work is only during term time, and as a part-timer you don't get paid during the long university holidays. This adds a scheduling challenge to your week, especially if you have to sort childcare or similar.

Probable income level

This will usually be an hourly rate – and probably different rates for different activities – so it will depend on how many hours you can/want to do. But once you're through the door, it's regular work.

How do you get started?

These jobs are competitive gigs, not usually advertised in the papers. You're going to need to know someone or make a call at the right time.

A great way to get started is to offer to give a guest lecture. Many programmes have space for a few guest lecturers towards the end of term, where you can talk about your business experience so students can get some real-world flavour. If you can manage to pull off a successful guest lecture, you've got a great opportunity to let the organiser know you'd love a more regular spot.

Having said this, if you've got the right type of CV and can get your foot just a little way through the door, more work may well come your way.

What it costs to get going

Nada – just you and your brain needed.

Top tip

If you're thinking this is something you'd like to do and you're still in your senior job in Corporate World, get started now. Get in touch with the course managers of local professional programmes at universities and let them know you're available to give a guest lecture. Then when you go out on your own and want to hit them for some regular work, they already know who you are.

Where to from here?

You can find all the UK's universities at www.dcsf.gov.uk – that's a start.

CASE STUDY

Interview: Karen Dickson, kinesiologist and clinical hypnotherapist

Karen's journey has taken her from a business consulting career with some of the world's biggest consultancies, to practising independently as a kinesiologist and clinical hypnotherapist.

'When I was young, I wanted to be a teacher but didn't get the marks. This was at the time when it was a really popular career choice and it was hard to get into. My father suggested computing instead as a growing industry, so I did a double degree in computing and accounting.

'Andersens, KPMG and a bunch of others came to the university and I ended up with six job offers! I took a management consulting position with Touche Ross, which was bought out here [in Australia] by KPMG, and then I moved to Andersens.

'I had a yearning for a job in the "real" world, so I took a job with a start-up company during the "dotcom boom". Six weeks there was like six months in a consultancy! It was life, speeded up. I was doing everything. I learned a lot about professionalism – well, actually, the lack of it in this business.

'Then I joined Freehills [corporate law firm] to help them commercialise a software product they'd developed for the Sydney Olympics.

'While I was there I saw a chiropractor who performed a small amount of kinesiology for stress management. It worked so well for me I developed a desire to study the underlying disciplines. So I took a year off for a kind of "time out" and found I was loving it, working with people and making changes at a really personal, intimate level.'

That led to a fascination with the human brain, which in turn led Karen to clinical hypnotherapy. It's not nearly as disconnected from her roots as you'd imagine: 'I'm working with the finest computer in the world – the human brain!' she says. 'It's like programming, helping people program their brains to achieve what they want in life.'

Karen talks about what psychologists call 'flow' – that experience of doing what's meant to be, being fully involved and engaged. 'When you find things hard and run into brick walls all the time, perhaps that's a sign that it's time to reflect on whether this is really what you're meant to be doing with your life,' she says. Instead, she suggests, when you take a single step in a direction that feels right to you, you'll find that the view changes and other options open up.

Benefits

1. When you tap into your passions, it doesn't matter how hard you have to work because you're doing what you love!
2. I was doing things to fulfil the expectations of others, not myself, and I think that's what led to the feeling of stress. Now I'm much more authentic – much more 'me', if you like.

Lessons

1. Do what you love and love what you do.
2. Temper that with wisdom: your ambition needs to be shaped by experience. You're not going to be mega-rich within two years!
3. The world is a great big place and there are lots of options. You don't need to be chained to your salary or your lifestyle.

Trades and services
What is it, exactly?

You're a sparkie. You're a plumber. You're a brickie. You're a carpenter. You're working for the man and you really, really want to stop. He's a git, and that's on a good day. (Amazing, isn't it – it's like we know him personally. We don't, fortunately.)

If you're a man working in some kind of management job, you may well have dreamed of going all tough and getting yourself a truck. We've met a university lecturer who retrained as an electrician (and now fixes things at his old university and earns easily twice as much). Retraining is not a short route though – so if this is your big idea, make sure you're thinking of taking on a trade you can competently (and legally) perform, such as gardening or handyman work.

It ticks the boxes if:

- you're **fully qualified** and know your way around town. You need to have a good feel for what you're doing; once you're the boss the buck really does stop with you;

- you've got the **tools and a big truck** to put them in.

What you need

The most important thing to have is business savvy. You're going to be quoting, getting deposits, billings, chasing funds, marketing. If you don't know where to begin, get yourself on a small business course. We're serious: what determines whether you make a go of this or not is not the work – you know you're great at the work and we fully believe you – but how well you run the business. We know tradesmen who are busy as anything but who are not going to be in business in two years time because they're clearly floundering on the commercial front.

In addition, a few decent jobs to start you off wouldn't be a bad idea.

Upside

Finally, there'll be no more git of a boss sending you to do the rubbish bits of the jobs! And all the cash comes to you.

Downside

Work really does come in fits and starts. Some days you'll be incredibly busy, on others you'll have nothing to do at all.

It's also possible that you'll need an apprentice to do your own rubbish jobs, liability insurance, paperwork and red tape by the yard.

The responsibility wears lots of people down. You go home and you take the worries with you. Soon you'll even start to understand why your old boss was such a git in the first place.

Probable income level

This is generally better than you'd get as an employee, but the risks are yours too.

How do you get started?

Having a big job or two to start you off helps with the investments such as liability insurance and tools. Don't steal the boss's work though – it's a small world and that's bad karma.

Business cards, a few referrals, maybe a flyer to shove through letter boxes and you're away.

What it costs to get going

Liability insurance is absolutely key!

You also need a range of tools and a vehicle to put them in, but try and build up your toolbag as you go along rather than buying expensive stuff you don't actually need. It's amazing how strong the temptation gets when there's a few quid in the bank to go out and blow the lot on a whizzbang new gizmo. Resist: be the bloke who does the best job with the worst tools, rather than the bloke who used to have his own business.

Top tips

Find a point of difference for your business and promote it. Be famous for something. Interested in environmental issues? Only hire women? (Note: never hiring women is not a point of difference, there are plenty of those businesses already!) No breakages, guaranteed? Whatever is different about you and your business, identify it and talk about it constantly. When someone is looking for a plumber in the Yellow Pages, you want them to give you a call because they are interested in green issues too.

More information

Go to www.businesslink.co.uk and click on 'Your business sector' down the bottom lefthand side. Follow the links.

Web business
What is it, exactly?

The Web follows completely different financial models from the real world. If you're thinking that people will pay to view content on your website, you are wrong my friend. It didn't work for Rupert Murdoch and it won't work for you. The Web starts out free to users and ends up free to users. It's very, very rare that anyone puts down their hard earned to access advice or information on a website. After all, it's all free somewhere else – so why would they pay you for it?

On the other hand, if you can create an incredibly compelling website that gets zillions of people hanging out there, you get to make money from advertising/sponsorship. Think Facebook. Think eBay. Second employee Jeff Skoll netted US $2bn-plus from a few years hard work at eBay and now spends his life developing social entrepreneurship and movies with a conscience. Easy isn't it? Well, maybe and maybe not.

Even a reasonably readable website can pick up enough readers to find sponsorship (for ads and clicks to other sites, usually) and bring in a modest income. But you'll need to do your research and talk to someone who knows what they're doing. With just a few competitors (i.e. the entire Internet), it's not easy to create a website that brings enough compensation to cover the time and investment you've put in. If you're doing it for fun, fine. If this is your business model, do be careful: don't over-extend yourself and be conservative, especially on costs.

Assuming you've neither invented Facebook nor come up with a model where people will pay to access your content, the next best way to make money on the Web is to sell stuff.

For the particular makeup of the Web, what works best is a specialised product and a geographically dispersed audience. In other words, you'll be catering to a wide geographic market. So there are enough customers out there to sustain your business, but they're not all local and they can't just pop in; they're spread all round the UK, or indeed the world.

By specialised product, we mean something you can't get on your local high street. The kind of things that tend to do well include:

- **boutique-type, high end items** such as designer clothing for adults and children, handbags, jewellery;

- **niche products** that wouldn't sell in a shop but have a market out there. For example, Susannah buys products from a website that caters for kids with allergies – badges and t-shirts in little person sizes that say 'STOP – don't feed me, I have an allergy'. Brilliant. She's also used a website that swaps maternity clothes. Also genius;

- **secondhand** and vintage stuff, sourced by the owner of the website;

- **big things**, where delivery is included – no one wants to lug stuff home.

And of course there's also general retail, DVDs and so on, over the Web for people who can't stand the high street. This is harder because you're competing with very large retail groups with branding, back up and buying power that you can't hope to come near.

Tap into your specialist market – advertise in community newsletters, get links to your site from theirs.

It ticks the boxes if:
- you understand how the Web works and what makes people spend money there. You don't have to be technical – you can hire that bit in;

- you realise that business online may have different drivers from business offline. But the same disciplines apply: you have to be serious about this, and run it like a real business (which is what it is).

What you need

Obvious really, you need a product you can sell online – books and clothes are good because they don't break. If your product is Venetian glass vases, you might need to think again.

Upside

You can start it on a shoestring from the kitchen table. As long as your site looks good, you're good. In addition, you can live anywhere – Spain or Skegness – and be in the heart of things.

Downside

You don't get to meet your customers so you don't get good feedback – just sales or not sales. It can also be pretty labour intensive mailing things (don't forget to include P&P costs!), and there's also the fact that there's absolutely no guarantee that this will work. You're up against the whole world, and there's a lot of competition springing up every day.

Probable income level

Aim for medium to high priced items – you have to sell a lot of cheap secondhand books to make serious money.

We're deliberately being downbeat here, because there are these unrealistic expectations that everyone can be an overnight dotcom billionaire. Don't be fooled. For every Brad Greenspan (MySpace), Mark Zuckerberg (Facebook), Pierre Omidyar (eBay) and Craig Newmark (Craigslist), there's a hundred thousand tech-head Toms (myknickknacks.com), Dicks (zitcentral.org) and Harries (bellybuttonlint.co.uk) slaving away and getting nowhere. (You can have any of those web addresses, by the way: amazingly, they're not yet taken.)

Still, this whole Web malarkey has really only just got going and there will be many, many more success stories. You may be one of them, at which point you can burn tenners and stick two fingers up at us.

How do you get started?

Frankly, if you need to be told then in all probability this isn't for you. You missed the boat by 15 years, when it was still possible to have an idea one day and retire rich the next. You need high quality technical skills (either your own or hired in), entrepreneurial instincts, low cunning and the willingness to work for a long time without getting paid. The founders of eBay worked 100 hours a week for years without getting a cent to become the overnight success story everyone remembers them for. It's the old, old story: if it sounds too good to be true, it usually is.

What it costs to get going

Pick a number – and perhaps you need to multiply it by a million. Impossible to say with this one, and we won't even try.

Top tip

Do your business on eBay, where you've got an instant audience, built-in ecommerce set up and no site build or maintenance costs. On the other hand, you have less control over the appearance and brand of your online shop, of course, plus you're really only a tenant, so in time you may want to get yourself sorted properly. But there's no better place to start selling.

More information

You can't beat Chris Anderson's *The Long Tail* (see www.thelongtail.com) for starters – a classic if you're new to the dynamics of the Web economy.

Party planning/direct sales
What is it, exactly?

Keen to work from home, have a flexible lifestyle and make money? At least superficially, this is the one for you. Direct sales is when you (or your friends) go direct to your customers. You know the routine: hey, you're my friend! *(Ah, that's sweet.)* Come to a party! *(Hurrah!)* And don't forget your wallet! *(Oh dear, I think I'm busy that night.)*

Despite a reputation that may be described as variable at best, party planning – hosting a party around a product where people buy stuff – is increasingly and, in fact, phenomenally popular. You might hear this kind of selling called MLM (multi-level marketing) or network marketing.

Think **homewares** (like Tupperware), **cookware, foodstuffs, health** and

natural products, skincare and **makeup, books, underwear, sex toys, cleaning products** (for tidying up after the previous party, perhaps), **women's clothes, kids' clothes...**

So how does it work? You sign up to get product and promotional support and training. You're not doing it all yourself; up the line from you there is head office support, and down the line you may choose to recruit and train other people, and then you get a slice of their action on top of what you do yourself.

Parties are hugely popular and tap into the new spirit of saving money in this Global Financial Crisis world (though often these products are at least as expensive as mid-range brands in the shops).

You can also peddle your wares at toddler groups, workplaces, schools, fairs, fundraiser events for charities and clubs, catalogue sales, through letterboxing and other channels your group might suggest to you. Some MLM companies are OK with you selling through eBay too.

As always, the standard Carey-Bowen word of warning: if the organisation you're with – or, more accurately, the party planner representing that organisation you're dealing with – talks little about how exactly it all works and too much about instant huge cash, holidays and new cars as bonuses, then be very careful. We're not saying instant riches don't happen. Yes, they can and indeed they do, but it takes really seriously hard work to get to that level. The rule, as ever, is simply this: if it sounds too good to be true, then it almost certainly is. Do your own maths: how many plastic boxes do you need to sell to make it worth their while to give you a new car? That's a *lot.*

It's also important to know that party planning is like gambling: do not, under any circumstances, get yourself in deeper than you can afford. We mean absolutely no offence to party planners, and if you're already one and are reading this feeling offended, then let us be absolutely clear. The great majority of people involved in owning party plan businesses and running party plan groups are fine, upstanding people just trying to make a quid. We salute you. It's just that there is the occasional scum-sucking pondlife out there who finds doing it by the book all too hard, and has succumbed to the temptation to make *their* quid at the expense of the unwary. Don't commit to huge amounts of stock upfront that you really can't afford, and don't shell out large amounts of upfront fees. Take it easy to begin with. Ask to speak to half-a-dozen of their satisfied party planners – and then really *do* talk to them. It's a pain and time-consuming and it makes you no money, but it could save you thousands. If your contact starts babbling about privacy laws and company policy as reasons why you can't talk to others, smile sweetly and move on. (Alternatively, say this: 'That's absolutely fine. I couldn't agree more. Here's my number, get them to call me.' See what happens.)

Another method is through catalogue sales – leaving catalogues on people's doorsteps and coming back on a set day hoping for orders. We've not heard many good things about this system, sorry to say.

It ticks the boxes if:

- you're social, outgoing, and not afraid to get in people's faces and sell stuff;

- you want to work evenings and weekends – perhaps you have family commitments or are a night owl. If you're looking for flexibility and fun part-time work, this could be your gig;

- you're a woman – almost always. Most men would rather eat their own faces off than do this.

What you need

First and foremost, you need lots of friends who are happy to buy stuff. You'll also want to have a car, because you'll be lugging round demo kits of stuff – at night too. The skin of a rhinoceros comes in handy as well.

Upside

- You get to make money in a social setting.

- There are heaps of groups to choose from, so you can pick a product you really love showing off.

- Good groups give you loads of support and training.

Downside

- Unsocial hours, in the sense that you give up your evenings and weekends, when people are available.

- Although you're an independent operator with no boss, you'll be tied into an existing set up – minimal setup costs, but you're basically rolling out a franchise recipe. And you're also working to a really specific (and proven) sales script, which you may regard as an upside or downside, depending on how you feel about such things.

- It's hard work setting up party after party, and hard core – sell, recruit, sell, recruit, sell.

- You may get pressure from your group to hold more and more events.

- Are you quite sure you want to spend your evenings manipulating your friends' friends into buying a mascara that costs £25?

Probable income level

This can be very good if you can pull it off well. Most groups offer around 25 to 35 per cent of sales plus bonuses as a starting point, plus a discount off the stuff you buy for yourself, which is handy if you like the products. It really depends on the time you put in and how good you are (but then what doesn't?).

How do you get started?

Often by being recruited, as you'll know if you've been to any of these parties (and if you're a woman aged 18 to 60, you've certainly been invited). We would also advise you to go to lots of parties from different groups to see which you like the smell of, before you join up.

What it costs to get going

You'll usually need to buy a demo kit – the merchandise and a script to get started showing it off. The cost will depend on the product – probably between 60 and 200 quid. It's also likely that you'll need to pay for catalogues, hostess and guest gifts, and add more items to the start kit of samples – all of which costs you, of course. But not as much as, you know, renting a shop; this is a good business option if you want to start out small, earn a bit extra, don't have cash.

Joining a group should also cover you for public liability insurance: check that out. (For one thing, it's a sign of how well run and reputable your group is.)

Top tip

The real money is made by recruiting other people to become sellers – you get a slice of their action from then on without the hard yards of making the sales yourself.

And make sure you like the person who recruits you – you'll get lots of help and support from them, so you want them to be someone you respect.

See the warning note above. Cut it out and glue it to the inside of your eyelids.

More information

There's an absolute stack of websites to look at. We won't recommend any in particular, since there is no association or independent body we're aware of, and everyone else is really there to push their own party plan business (which is fair enough). Just Google 'party plan' and start working your way through the lists. Don't be put off by garish and untidy sites and, indeed, don't be overly impressed with a good looking site either: having a good site design and being professional aren't necessarily the same thing.

There are some excellent books (and some godawful ones, too) on the subject at www.amazon.co.uk.

Any other business

Yes, we admit it: a catch-all section for everything else. (Plus we got to say 'Any other business' which made us ex-Corporate Meeting jockeys chuckle. No? Oh please yourself.)

In this chapter we've considered a few options. What we haven't done is to pretend that this exhausts your options. Lordy no, far from it. (Here's a bit of useless trivia for you: the North American Industrial Classification System of Businesses identifies 1,170 industries, from accounting, acting and advertising (copywriter) all the way through wood television, radio and sewing machine cabinet manufacturing – we kid you not – to yarn texturising and youth services. It's worth a look if you're stuck.[6]) Where would catering and cooking fit? Or personal training, or that odd nineties phenomenon, life coaching? What about all the allied and alternative health professions, such as acupuncture and chiropractic and clinical hypnotherapy and herbalism and massage and naturopathy and osteopathy? What about writing, the slow boat to poverty? Or owning a hotel or bed-and-breakfast place? Or the aforementioned wood television, radio and sewing machine cabinet manufacturing (so good we named it twice)?

Here's a job for you, as it were: next time you're out, count how many different types of potential self-employed businesses there are between your home and the city. Now tell us you can't think of any options.

---

[6] www.smallbusinessnotes.com/businesses/alphabusinesses/complete.html

BUSINESSES YOU CAN START ON UNDER £200

Some businesses take a lot of cash – a *lot* of cash. Buying a franchise, or indeed buying any business, costs big time. Even buying a taxi-plate doesn't come cheap.

But what if you don't have a cracker? Does that mean you're out of the game? Not at all. You have your hands and that's a start; even better if you have the gift of the gab to go with them.

So if you have the skills of any of the following, plus you have an ability to talk the hind leg off a donkey, you are – quite literally – in business:

- beautician
- copyeditor/writer
- gardener
- handyman
- home organiser
- massage therapist
- naturopath
- painter (portraits)
- painter (walls)
- personal trainer
- photographer
- zillions of other personal services or trades

Now for some types of activity you need a qualification, insurance, and/or a licence, and that's not a bad thing in our book. So wherever your skills lie, make sure you check out any legal requirements. As always, www.businesslink. co.uk is a great jumping-off point, and has a great section on compliance requirements (high-falutin' talk for paperwork).

Some professions lend themselves to freelance work, such as:

- accountant
- architect
- business consultant
- financial adviser

- graphic designer
- marketing consultant
- psychologist
- specialist teacher (music, languages)
- Web designer

Re-training to become one of these, if you are currently doing something different altogether, is a lengthy process – that's not what we're suggesting at all. But whatever your profession or trade, could you start your own business? For many of us the answer is absolutely – with a decent computer, a business card and a sign up in the local supermarket, you can get a few gigs to get you started and build up from there. For many of these you can work from home and travel to your customers' premises – so you don't need a public office space.[7] Easy. This is not necessarily to say you'll make a living wage straight away, but with not much investment you can pick up work on the weekend to supplement your income and in not much time at all you'll be able to see if you've got enough momentum to really get into it.

Are you a reasonably senior manager – sales, marketing or general business? **Business consulting**, surprisingly perhaps, isn't a regulated industry: anyone can hang their shingle up and start tomorrow without knowing what they're doing, and judging by some we've seen, that's indeed about the degree of their expertise. But for many of us (yes, we fit into this category) a lifetime of corporate experience is great training to help other businesses that need a hand. It's indoor work with no heavy lifting, and if you work through a reputable organisation like the one Steve's with, the Institute for Independent Business (www.iib.ws), you can find yourself a ready-made network. (Admittedly this fails the 200 quid test by quite a few thousand, but you needn't join this or any group until you've got yourself going. So we'll let it through on a technicality.)

If you're a wheeler-dealer type, you can set yourself up as an **eBay trader**, establishing a 'virtual store' that grows at exactly the pace you

---

[7] Please be careful if you're travelling to your customers' premises, especially if it's their home and especially if you're a woman.

dictate. This is a perfect business to start if you've got little cash and lots of expertise about what sells into a specialist market for more than most people realise. Scouring car boot sales and charity shops and second-hand shops, cleaning things up and reaching a niche market where someone will love the items – lots of fun. Unless you hit a goldmine no one else has thought of, it will take you a while to build momentum and make big money. But find your niche and there is certainly a living to be had if you're particularly good at it. (In fact, apply all the business principles we talk about throughout this book and you'll find you're a good deal better than many in cyberspace, which does attract its fair share of the self-deluding, the ill-at-ease and general nutbaggery.)

If you're crafty by nature, get **making things**. Take a stall at farmers' and craft markets and sell candles, jewellery, crafts, knick-knacks of whatever kind you can make or source that takes your fancy. If your things look professional rather than homemade, you may also be able to sell through independent retailers. Again, you need to excel at the marketing side of things to make a living out of this. You need to know who your customers are, for one thing, and have a product that appeals at a price that sells. You need to have a good location at which to sell, but without paying over the odds so that you go out backwards within the first couple of weeks. And the hide of a rhinoceros is useful, to bear all that passing traffic of puzzled punters who can't imagine why they'd be interested in what you have to offer.

Wrangling with babies and children is not a bad way to get going. Good nannies/mother's helpers are always in demand so if you know your way around the little people and you are honest, responsible and sober, you'll find people who trust you with theirs. Formal qualifications are not required to nanny in the UK, though you'll want to do a First Aid course and be able to prove experience. Get recommendations to find a good agency to help you pick up work.

Walking dogs and minding pets for holidaymakers is a bit casual with cash, but perfect for a spot of top-up work while you plan your empire. Neither will make you rich, but can be the first steps to entrepreneurial heaven. Could your poodle washing activities be the start of a beautiful franchise? You won't know until you try!

If you've got a small truck at your disposal, maybe you can become a (wo)man with a van and start a **furniture removal** company?

Catering is an obvious area of interest if you like to get out the wooden spoons. Can you make delightful cupcakes for special occasions, or sell sandwiches for office lunches? Be careful – this is an area that's highly regulated (and three cheers for that, speaking as your potential customers), so you're going to need to register your premises (even if you're cooking at home) and follow lots of guidelines. The Food Standards Agency has a superb brochure, 'Starting up: your first steps to running a catering business'. Search for 'catering' at www.businesslink.gov.uk. Once you've got over those hurdles, you need some basic equipment, but if you start out simply (biscuits in three or four shapes, for example) you can build up from there.

Party planning is an obvious starting point if you need to start with a little bit of cash but want to tap into a proven business. The small starter kits can help you start out modestly, and as you build up you can invest in more samples and so on.

CASE STUDY

Interview: Andrew Wozencroft, gardener

Andrew trained as a secondary school teacher, taught history for a number of years and now runs a gardening business.

'After university I earned some cash as a factory worker and farmhand. I travelled a bit and moved to London and worked as a gardener at the Royal Parks for four years. Then I decided to become a teacher, so I moved home and studied some more and taught for ten years. Four years ago I set up a gardening maintenance business.

'I miss the holidays of being a teacher! I miss the interaction with kids. I don't miss teachers though – most of them do my head in.

'I set up the business because I wanted to work for myself. I was just sick of the bureaucracy and the fact that I couldn't just teach, I constantly had to put in place new government policy and paperwork and so on.

'I chose gardening because it's something I like – I like going into situations which are disorganised and walking away knowing I've improved matters. I love working the hours I want to work and doing the jobs I want to do. It's great to earn an income through doing something you enjoy.

'The business aspects are hard. I find it difficult to quote for jobs – it's tricky to assess how much time is needed. I'm not a good businessman, I don't like ripping people off. I'm not hardnosed, so if anything I underestimate on quotes. And a lot of people I work for are people I know through someone, so I always tend to undercharge them.

'The bookwork isn't great. Taxation and public liability insurance, for example, require a lot of paperwork.

'The other thing is all time has to be productive. You can't have any downtime – it's a cost to you. When you work for someone else, you don't have to be productive all the time because you're getting paid anyway – your time isn't so measured. For example, if I move between two jobs I lose an hour in travelling. I maintain my tools, I go home and do my bookwork. As an employee, if you travel between jobs it's all part of your income. When you work for yourself you have to factor that into your hourly rate.

'What advice would I offer someone thinking about doing this?

1. **It has to be something you really enjoy doing,** that you believe in, that you're passionate about. It absorbs so much of your time. A business can only be successful if a person is committed to the product. If you're passionate about it you have a high degree of understanding of the product, and that makes the business better.
2. **Start small and make do.** Don't go and buy all the latest gizmos and gear. Just buy things as you go along, as you increase your client base.
3. **Whatever jobs you get initially, do them and do them well,** maybe even make a loss if you have to, because you build a reputation that way. If you mess up your first jobs and get people offside, that reputation will hinder the growth of your business.

'I think to be an independent business person you have to be more driven and more independent – you're doing it on your own and you don't have a fallback option, you don't have other people to bounce ideas off. And you don't have a marketing or an accounts department, at least initially. You do everything, so you're much more of an all-rounder.

'Theoretically I would go back and get a job again, as a teacher or in a big business. I think it's easier to separate work and home life when you work for someone else, and I miss that. There's always something to do when you work for yourself. And the backup of having guaranteed income, guaranteed sick days, a good pension – all those things offer a real benefit.'

Conclusion: mash it up

One last point about all these fabulous options: where is it written that you have to restrict yourself to one thing at a time? You can keep your job (yuk), at least for the time being, and start your business; you can run two or three businesses simultaneously and see what works.

If you're a fresh escapee from Corporate World, you're probably used to having one job and that's the job you do. It doesn't have to be like that here in Please Yourself World! For example:

- Susannah teaches at university (one day), does research and training and business consultancy (three days), freelance writing (evenings) and has two young kids (priceless).

- Steve is a business adviser (three days); publishing industry specialist (one day); university lecturer (two days in term) – this shifts around, depending on what's hot and what's not, of course; and a clinical hypnotherapist (one day).

- Andrew teaches (five days) and runs a gardening business (two days). Sometimes he just gardens (five or six days) or teaches a bit and gardens more.

- Anthony consults to business (three days) and runs a gym (four days).

- Leisa is a personal trainer (six days) and hosts a cooking show on pay TV (half of Wednesday).

Notice anything (apart from our incredible talent and good looks, of course)? That's right: we're all ridiculously heavily, and perhaps even over, committed. Although we would each claim to have a good degree of work-life balance, the fact of the matter is that we love what we do and none of us is yet a millionaire. We work hard and long, and wouldn't want you to think otherwise. If it's the easy life you're after, think again.

(On the other hand, we do have the wonderful luxury of dropping off our kids or picking them up or being there when there's something important on. Lots of suits never get that chance.)

This emphasis on variety and multiple roles may appear flatly to contradict advice we give elsewhere in this book, suggesting that one of the biggest faults we entrepreneurs have is that we tend to spot opportunities everywhere, and in trying to grab hold of them as we rush through, drop the whole bundle.

Well, both are true. You may well achieve a portfolio of different things that you run together, and that's fine – for one thing it spreads the risk, and as that part over there takes off and this bit dies down, you can go with the flow (and more importantly go with the cash). On the other hand, you do need to be aware of the dangers of over-committing yourself.

The golden rule is probably simply this: if you spot an opportunity that you passionately believe in, commit yourself wholeheartedly to it to the extent you can afford to. By all means keep up the 'banker' aspect of your portfolio, so you've got your bills covered and perhaps also are generating some revenue to plough into your dream.

What we've seen happen too many times, and what we're warning you to be on your guard against, is that tendency to be a serial faller-in-love: you're convinced that this is The One, the opportunity you've been waiting for all your life, the one you can't afford to pass by. So you drop absolutely everything else and seize it…only to find, just weeks later, something else even shinier and more attractive crops up. There's a real danger here, because it's true what the Richard Bransons and Alan Sugars say: there are heaps of opportunities out there. Once you get the knack of adjusting your eyesight so you can see them, they appear everywhere.

Which is fine. The trouble comes, though, if you're the type of person who's prone to the business equivalent of getting all caught up in skiing one season, then scuba-diving the next, then cycling, then abseiling…you know the type? That's all very well and good in your leisure time (who are we to say otherwise?), but it's an awful recipe for building personal wealth.

It's a cliché, but (as the cliché about clichés has it) it's only a cliché because it's true: stick to the knitting.

CHAPTER SEVEN

WILL IT WORK?

> Running a successful business is simpler (not easier, but simpler!) than I thought. Competition is easily eliminated when you deliver what you promise. What surprised me? How FEW businesses are actually thriving. Most are just 'getting by'. Carl Gould, CMT International

Leaving the nest

For someone used to the undoubted benefits of working for someone else – the regular salary, the structure, the expenses, the regular salary, the potential for career development, the regular salary – striking out on one's own can seem pretty intimidating. Good. You *should* feel intimidated, because it's all new and fresh and different from what you're used to. You'd be a strange beast indeed if it didn't seem daunting.

There are two ways to reduce this feeling of daunt. The first is to crack on and do it anyway, prove to yourself that you can do it and discover in doing so that actually, as so often, the fear is much worse than the reality could ever be. The second, which is to read this chapter, has the distinct advantage that you can have it done over the weekend.

What we're going to do is to reduce this sense of a big and overwhelming task by breaking into in a number of smaller and, therefore, less over-whelming tasks. As they say, the best way to eat an elephant is mouthful by mouthful. The purpose of eating *this* elephant, becoming a successful self-employed business owner, should at least be obvious.

Here's what we find most people are a wee bit daunted about, before stepping out on their own:

1. money or, more accurately, the lack thereof;
2. whether they're up to it;
3. whether the reality lives up to their dream.

Let's take those three concerns one by one.

1. Show me the money

It's the money, isn't it? Above all, it's the money. It's going from the certainty and security of a regular pay cheque, paid holidays and sick leave and contributions to your pension scheme, to the uncertainty and lack of security of having to live off the sweat of your own brow – or go hungry.

Somehow, knowing that no one has a job for life any more and that the apparent security of full-time employment is just as much a chain around your neck doesn't make it much easier to give up. Perhaps, you might say to yourself, it's best to leave it for another year, by which time you'll have that much more put aside and things may sort themselves out – and if they don't then that's the time to start thinking about the options.

Yes, probably. If that's how you feel, you're probably right. It's a judgement call and no one else is in a position to make it for you.

However, it may be worth bearing a few things in mind:

- **Next year is rarely the right time** to have kids, decide to get married or take that year off you've always promised yourself. Why? Because for most of us it's *never* the right time to do these things. Unless you're a very disciplined and focused individual, your circumstances in a year's time are unlikely to be so much better that the wait's been worth it.

- You really, really, *really* don't want to be trying to set up your own business without **the security of a job** and the certainty of a pay cheque at the end of the month. Now this sounds contradictory, because we've just been saying that there's no good reason to put this off till next year. But in fact there's all the difference in the world between thinking that you're going to put off till next year the making of a plan; and the making of a plan now that means you are going to quit next year (on Friday 24 September at 11:32 a.m.) and have something to go to.

- **It's worth pointing out what you already know:** the security is illusory. Certainly there's no loyalty from your employer, who will fire you like a shot if circumstances require it. You'd do the same thing yourself in the same circumstances. So it would be unwise to depend upon the apparent safety you currently enjoy, even if at the moment things look pretty rosy. At the very least, it'd be good to have a Plan B.

- **People adapt to income and lifestyle very, very quickly.** Hopefully this'll mean learning to adapt upward, where your houses and cars and things get bigger; but if you need to adapt downward for a year or two, is that the worst thing in the world? Remember when you were at university and waitressing to make ends meet. Your annual income then was probably less than you pay now in tax. Look at your spend now compared to then – there are almost certainly areas where you can cut back (and may be cutting back anyway, due to the credit crunch).

- **Anyway, who are we kidding?** You're knee deep in a book all about how to quit your corporate gig and start up a business for yourself, so there's no point in pretending you're not thinking seriously about it. OK, so you're weighing up the benefits and, at least for the time being, certainties of paid employment against the risk of giving all that up and doing your own thing. We know that. And the money really is quite a big thing to get over.

So here are a couple of things that you may not yet have considered that need to be part of your decision-making:

- **A pound isn't a pound.** A pound earned as an employee is not the same as a pound you earn for yourself out of your own business. If you work from home, for example, you can claim tax relief, and if you need a car to run the business, you probably won't have to own another one for your own private use. Best thing is to talk to your accountant, or talk to someone who is already self-employed. You'll find that some of the difference between the high salary you earn as an employee and the lower gross income you'll probably be pulling in at the start of your own business venture will disappear – not all of it, certainly, but probably a good chunk of it.

- **There is no amount of money in the world that can compensate you for having a miserable life.** If you're working desperately long hours and/or are under extreme pressure from a job that makes excessive demands upon you, then the fact that you're making a lot of money is not, in our view, enough to make up for it. (And believe us, we know whereof we speak.) And while you may agree with us in theory, the fact is that many people, in practice, live their lives as if this weren't true: they put up with – pardon our French – a shit sandwich because of the bread. Are you one of them?

- *Are* **you getting rich anyway?** Maybe you are, and if that's the case then congratulations and please move smartly and smugly to the next point. Most of us don't really get that rich out of employment. Maybe we live in a nice big house (though curiously it's never *quite* big enough… funny, that) and take holidays in pleasant sunny places (though curiously it's never *quite* the holiday we'd really love to have). And while survey after survey demonstrates that we say (and perhaps even believe) that money doesn't make us happy, we certainly don't behave as if we believe this to be true.

- The converse is also true: **lack of money doesn't make you unhappy.** Admittedly having so little money that you can't eat can get to be a bit of a drag after a while, but we're probably not talking about that kind of poverty. We're talking about the kind of lack of money that only makes you unhappy *if you decide that you should be.* Fundamentally it is not our circumstances that make us happy or sad: it's what we make of them. Stands to reason. Otherwise the world's richest man would be the happiest, and the world's poorest the unhappiest, with everyone neatly lined up depending on income. Unlikely. So if you consciously and firmly decide that you really would rather have your own business than work for someone else, then that, of course, is what matters to you. As Jimmy Cliff put it, 'I'd rather be free man in my grave/Than living as a puppet or a slave.' (Actually, perhaps that's not such a great quote, especially the bit about the grave and all. But what we think he was getting at was that while freedom may come at a price, it's a price worth paying.)

- **One last thing:** even if your monthly take-home goes down as you get your business moving, the longer-term earning potential of being an entrepreneur can be significantly greater than being an employee. As an employee, you may get bonuses and stock options and reliability and all that. As a business owner, you are at the top of the tree and your earning potential is where you want it to be. To put it another way, Richard Branson probably wouldn't own an island if he were working a management job in the City.

2. Whether you're up to it: do you really have the right stuff?

Some people – and perhaps more than will readily admit it – have doubts about their own ability to pull this off. Doesn't it take some kind of special person to create a business from scratch? Certainly if you read a lot of the books about launching businesses, you'd imagine this to be the case. You've got to be brilliant, they say; you need a real passion and flair for sales and marketing, they say; you need to be able to do the accounting and compliance stuff, they say. In fact, you need to have something a bit special running through your veins to be an entrepreneur. Hell, even the word 'entrepreneur' sounds pretty pumped up, doesn't it, as if there's a board somewhere that decides whether you can call yourself one. It smacks of 25-year-old Silicon Valley billionaires (and smacks are what they deserve, little bastards).

Good thing you bought our book really, instead of (or as well as) all those other books.

Instead, think of all the people you've met or had some connection with in the past week who have done just what we're describing. The bloke who runs the corner shop where you bought milk. The painter or electrician you got to quote for you. The owner-operator of your kids' nursery. The young fellow who runs the computer shop that has PCs with games on that your kids play with. These are all small business owners. Some are doing a great job, while others are not. Very few will have put together the detailed planning that you're putting into this project right now.

Of course, it's not true to say that *any* old person can launch a business, particularly a successful and thriving one. It certainly does require a reasonable level of creativity, intelligence, ambition and sheer hard work that not everyone can deliver. For those who jump into this without having the requisite talent in these areas, it can be a pretty miserable experience.

However, it's unlikely that you are short of any of these requirements. For one thing, you're reading this book, so you clearly have access to some great resources. (We're not pumping up our own tyres here, just pointing out that people who can find their way to good resources such as these are unlikely to be without a good deal of business background.)

To reveal our hand here, we think any fairly intelligent, thoughtful and passionate person is capable of launching a business – on three conditions:

1. **They really, really want to.** This is no place for someone who's just playing around.
2. **They are willing to learn.** If you haven't done this before, learn from those who have. If you have done it before, learn from those who have done it more than you. Never stop learning.
3. **They believe in themselves.** We'll talk about this shortly, but it is vital that you have confidence. As Henry Ford said, 'If you think you can or think you can't, you're probably right.'

3. Whether the reality lives up to your dream

Finally, one little-discussed reason people put off doing something that's important to them is that they fear it won't live up to its billing. It's as if they are so afraid of risking disappointment that it's almost better not to confront the possibility.

Well, that's understandable at a subconscious level, and it's worth looking inside yourself to check whether that's the case with you. If it is, you need to work on it – which is to say, you have to recognise it, describe it (write down how you feel) and confront it. Ask yourself whether there are reasons why you're not pursuing something that is, so it seems, very important to you.

Then ring your therapist.

Just kidding! After all, every person walking this planet is a big mix of complex and sometimes conflicting mental processes. Nothing wrong with having sophisticated emotions – as long as you're not being held back unnecessarily. If you are, think about whether it's worth sorting it out – on your own or with help.

So...will it work?

In this new venture of yours, there is no room for certainty. Of that you can be quite...certain. However you imagine it, the reality will turn out very different – better in some ways, worse in others, but in general just *different*.

And since that's the case – that it's not going to be how you imagine it – then *how* you imagine it becomes at once both less important and more important. Less, because it's not an accurate depiction of what will, in fact, happen; and more, because how you imagine things affects how you feel and you need to feel at your best to be at your best.

So, a paradox. We're going to argue two entirely different and apparently contradictory lines. We want you to think both this:

- **Will it work? *Of course* it will!**

And at the very same time, think this, too:

- **Can I guarantee it? *Of course* I can't!**

Somehow you've got to behave as if you can't fail; and at the same time be acutely aware at every moment that there's the possibility that you can indeed fail.

Here's what we're saying. Even in the absence of a guarantee from us (and you didn't really expect one, did you?), it makes a lot of sense, if you're going to do this at all to develop a very positive, gung ho confidence that it damn well *will* be a success, come hell or high water.

It makes sense to think this way for three reasons. The first is that, in some curious way that sounds all hippy and ridiculous if pressed too hard, you really do get out of life what you look for. Misery loves company and all that. If you go around expecting failure and disappointment, you will get those very things. We've all met those people who just 'know' this can't possibly work or that will be a disaster – and they're usually right. If you go to the party expecting not to meet anyone interesting, you'll come home confirmed in your belief. And yet if you are absolutely convinced that it'll be a good party, that there's bound to be someone there worth talking to, the chances are you'll find them and come home pleased that you went.

The second reason is about the fun you have on the road. You'll enjoy the trip more if you are positive and optimistic and genuinely believe it can and will work out.

We are aware of the other side of the coin, that if you set yourself up for success and it doesn't work out then you'll be disappointed. Well bollocks to that, frankly, and pardon us for the rough language – but really, what codswallop. Will you somehow be *less* disappointed if things don't work out if you were expecting disaster all along? We don't think so. We just think you'll end up being a misery guts along the way and that's no fun at all, for yourself or for anyone around you.

The fact is, the future hasn't happened yet and doesn't exist anywhere except in your head. That being the case, why would you choose to imagine a future reality that's full of unhappiness and failure when you can just as easily picture one that is full of happiness and success?

There's a third reason, too, and it's this: you deserve success and you deserve happiness. Much of the time, it seems to us, people (and particularly British people) beat themselves up because they're somehow less deserving of success than others, for reasons never made sufficiently clear[8]. And in beating themselves up, they actually manage to deprive themselves

---

[8] Of course, there's the other set, too, those who honestly believe that they do deserve success but don't have to do anything to achieve it – it's owed to them, for some reason they never quite get around to explaining. We know you're not like that, or you wouldn't be reading this particular book, so we won't dwell on that peculiar tendency.

of their best opportunity to enjoy the success they crave. They make it less likely to happen (because their belief ends up being self-fulfilling) and they manage not to enjoy whatever degree of success they meet along the way (because they don't deserve it and therefore don't even recognise it as success when it happens).

Anyway, why *not* you? That's right, why not you? If Richard and Rupert and Anita and Alan and Donald, why not you? You do deserve to be successful and, yes, rich, do you not? Yes you do.

That, then, addresses the first half of the paradox – the 'Will it work? *Of course* it will!' half. There is also, however, the other half – the 'Can I guarantee it? *Of course* I can't!' half. If it makes sense to proceed with confidence and enthusiasm (because it sure as hell beats the alternative), then it does also make sense to remain aware that success is not assured. After all, if you genuinely *did* start to believe that you couldn't fail and that success was a certainty, then it wouldn't matter whether you tried or not, would it? You may as well take the afternoon off and play golf – this thing is in the bag, so why worry? No, that won't work, of course. And that's why the absence of a guarantee is the best thing you can have, the thing that keeps you grinding away and working your very hardest to give yourself the best possible chance of success.

Four in five businesses fail in their first year...or do they?

If you've already told people what you plan to do, it's virtually certain you'll have had this statistic, or one very like it, quoted back at you. And if you haven't yet told people what you plan to do, be prepared to hear this as part of their response. It isn't, frankly, all that welcome a statistic, yet somehow there's always someone who feels obliged to quote it at you. Actually it often appears to be stated by those who are jealous, who wish it was them having a crack rather than you. Otherwise, we're just not at all clear why your friends, family, colleagues and acquaintances would want to feed you such a pearl of wisdom.

Neither are we at all sure that it's true. We would dearly love to know the source of this alleged statistic – and it certainly takes the wind out of people's sails when they spout it and you ask them where they got their information.

You may sweetly point out to them that it's a well-known fact that 74 per cent of all statistics are made up and you suspect, though you don't know for sure, that this may be one of them, and if they could possibly get you the source you'd love to see it, because you've been on the hunt for it for years now and still haven't found it...

It may well be the case that most business names registered don't go on to lead long and productive lives (hell, we've registered a few in our time that have fallen by the wayside), but if that is the source, it's a long way from saying that most businesses that get up and running and trading keel over within their first 12 months.

However, even if it *is* true, what does it actually mean? Might it mean, for example, that most businesses set up by people who haven't prepared a business plan, don't have a vision, don't have sufficient working capital, haven't thought it through properly and are actually just flying on a wing and a prayer crash and burn ignominiously within their first year? Because if that *is* the case, we don't see the relevance. *Your* business isn't like that, is it? You *do* (or soon will) have a business plan and a vision and sufficient working capital, and you *have* thought this through, haven't you? That, after all, is the whole point of this book. So why anyone would imagine that the viability or otherwise of businesses that go off half-cocked and never stand a chance of succeeding have anything to do with what you're doing, we do not know and frankly do not care.

Even so, whatever the statistics, there *are* failures – perhaps more failures than successes (though we don't have a source for that guess). So it does make sense to acknowledge and understand that success is not certain and that failure is a possibility. However, businesses fail for many different reasons, and while you can't eliminate all the possibilities, you can certainly improve your chances considerably (see Chapter 14 on improving your odds). What you must aim to do is to address all the ways in which your venture can fail – and then stop worrying.

And with regard to the ways your venture could fail and the difficulties you'll face along the way (even as it succeeds), here's a tip. Assume that there will be something like six, or perhaps 16 or even 66, rocks on your road – difficulties that must be overcome before you get to your Promised

Land. That means, therefore, that each obstacle you hit means you've now encountered one more of the 66 you will come across – and that means one less to deal with in future. Put in this way, it may even be possible not exactly to welcome these difficulties, but to meet them head on and acknowledge them for what they are: necessary steps on the road to your success.

A word about your self-belief

And that brings us round to an issue which we've already touched on earlier in this chapter: your self-belief. You need to know whether you're good at this or not. If you typically expect to succeed at what you do and are always surprised when things don't work out, then you have high self-belief. If, however, you expect that it's all going to go horribly wrong and that if it hasn't yet, it's just a question of time until the natural order reasserts itself and the whole pack of cards comes tumbling down, then you have high self-belief in your ability to make a mess of things.

We doubt, personally, that there's a high correlation between good self-belief and expectation of success and actually succeeding; nor between high self-belief in one's ability to muck it up and actually mucking it up. It's more about how you see the future. And as we pointed out earlier, since the future has not yet been written it makes little sense to imagine it negatively.

Yes, we know, you don't actually set out to imagine a bleak future: it just seems to present itself that way. And we're not saying you can easily change this stuff. What we are saying is that being aware of your tendency to paint it black (or white) is useful knowledge, as is being aware that we're all pretty terrible at predicting the future anyway.

So what flows out of this? Three things:

1. **Don't beat yourself up.** Whether it's a tendency to take a bleak view of how things are likely to turn out, or a tendency to beat yourself up, don't beat yourself up about it. Just accept that's how you are, work on it as much as you can and shrug your shoulders. None of us is perfect.
2. **Don't take it lying down.** You can change outlook, if you work on it, and while you shouldn't give yourself too much of a hard time, you should

keep reminding yourself that, over time and with a fair amount of hard work, you can improve your track record on this stuff.

3. **Work on behaviour, not attitude.** We smile when we're happy; it's also well demonstrated that we feel happy when we smile. If you know you've a tendency to take the black view, try just to get on with it. Don't give in to the feeling and, if you're able to keep going, do so. However, if you do find yourself sinking under the weight of it all, don't hesitate to go and get help. It's not a sign of weakness, it's a sign of strength. If you broke a leg you'd go to the doctor, so if you get broken on the inside, do the same – he or she'll help you get back on track. You can save yourself a lot of misery this way.

And a word about fear

Finally, for this chapter, we'd like to touch on the things that have the power to stop you that aren't business related. The current global financial crisis is one thing and certainly a factor to be considered. A much more powerful factor, frankly, is your own fear and how it drives you to do certain things – and prevents you from doing certain things.

You're probably already aware of a **fear of failure**. No one wants to take on a big project like this and end up with it all turning to dust in their hands. You don't want the financial loss and you don't want the loss of face. That's entirely natural, and in fact a fear of failure drives many of the world's richest men. It certainly continued to drive Australian billionaire Kerry Packer right up till he died. You'd imagine it's driving Rupert Murdoch, who's been close to the edge more than once or twice, while Bill Gates famously talked about how paranoia was what drove Microsoft to greater and greater heights. So it can be a powerful and productive force.

Just as likely, and much less expected, is the power of the **fear of success**. We touched on this above, when we mused upon the fear we all have that success won't be what we'd hoped for. It's that old sense of 'be careful what you wish for', that notion that the worst thing that can happen is to get what you're after. For one thing, what do you do for an encore? And, even more pressingly, what will it feel like if you spend massive amounts of time and energy in getting something, only to find that it's not what you want after all?

There is also the **fear of being unable to cope**. Are you the right person? Can you handle it? Will it all prove too much for you? And in which case, isn't it better not to grow too fast or go too high, in case it all flies apart? Getting out of control is a fear many of us have and this is a form of it.

Finally, many of us have **unhealthy attitudes towards money**. For various reasons, we believe that we're not entitled to it, or that it's dirty, or that you can't have money and maintain your integrity…all kinds of crazy notions which, put as nakedly as this, we recognise for what they are. However, they are buried deep down, where we can't easily get at them.

It's beyond the scope of this book to deal in great depth with these emotions and attitudes. However, you need to be aware that they may be operating within you and that, if they are, they will prove strong factors in limiting the extent of your success and even your prospects of success. All we can suggest is either some solid introspection, which not all of us are particularly good at, combined with some deep discussions with your nearest and dearest and perhaps delving into the realms of psychology. Alternatively, you can accept that you are as you are and just get on with it. We're not aware of any evidence that supports either approach as the better one, though our instinct is that somehow just being aware of such things seems somehow to help. At any rate, knowing what makes you tick is unlikely to do you any harm.

CHAPTER EIGHT

RESEARCHING YOUR OPTIONS

> **What surprised me? The ever-increasing delight of working with people you really respect and LIKE; the warm response the industry has to a small start-up newcomer; how much fun promotion is when it's your own beast you're unleashing.** Rose Michael, Arcade Publications

> **I was struck by how sometimes things that are second nature to one can be new and inspirational to others. How many people are in the same situation and how supportive they can be. And how much fun you can have!** Alison Richardson, Richardson Associates

So now you know what you want to do with the rest of your life – or at least the next part of it. Excellent. Well done. Without that step, there can be no journey. Now there's just the little matter of moving forward.

While we're figuring that one out, tell the love of your life, or whatever good friend is standing nearby when the mood hits you:

I'm going to become a kids' party host/personal trainer/mobile chef!
[Your selection here. Don't say them all at once or you'll scare the poor dear.]

Try on this new role like a new suit and see how it feels. If you can't say what you're going to do with a straight face, even to your nearest and dearest, or indeed if they burst out laughing and still haven't stopped, then perhaps you need to look again at this whole project (or get a new best friend).

Assuming that goes well, now get the research underway.

What you need to know

Start a new folder on your computer and create files for each of the ideas below (or if you prefer the old fashioned way, grab a bunch of manila folders). If you're nice and organised now, in years to come you can look back at this stuff and get all nostalgic about when you were starting out.

Six things you're going to need to know

Identify the questions that worry you more than the others. Spend more time on them. And remember, there won't be definite yes/no answers to this stuff – it's about doing your research, keeping your mind open and finding the right path for you.

First we're going to talk you through what you might want to find out and then look at research tips – how to actually find the information.

1. How do you **get started** in this field?

How do most people start out and how do the successful people start out? Do they just, well, start, or do they all work for one of the three big companies first? Do they work from the kitchen table and then open an office, or do they rent an office and hire staff? Do they wait until they have their first big job and then get into it, or get moving without a job/client? And do you have to do it that way too, or is it time to break the mould and start out differently?

2. Do you need formal **qualifications**?

Yes, if you're planning on being an accountant or architect; maybe not if you'd like to be a kitchen designer or gardener (though obviously you will want to know what you're doing, and training may be a good way of enhancing and formalising your experience).

3. If so, what? And where is the **best place** (best reputation, best teaching, best course) for you to get those qualifications?

You'd be astonished at how many people start studying and then realise it's not what they want or doesn't give them what they need. Big fat waste of time and money! Think about any course you've ever done. Ever wondered about all the people who don't make it to the end? They should probably never have started, to be honest.

Top things to do, then, *before* you start studying:

- **Make sure you really need to do the course** – whether because qualifications are essential or you feel you need the confidence and knowledge boost. If you're only doing it because you feel you should, it probably won't work out and it certainly won't be much fun, which after all is the point of this whole exercise.

- **Make sure you're doing the right course.** Is it as specialised as you need? Is it too specialised, which might lock you into a small part of your field? Does it cater enough to your specific interest? Have you checked to make sure there isn't a better course for you, a bit further away? Is the course overly theoretical, when you need something practical? Is it as a university or college that has a good reputation in your area or a good brand name? Are the staff friendly, available and still working in the field? Or are there heaps of students and you'll feel like you're just one of the sausages in the factory? Will you meet people you'll like and might be able to set up a business with?

See below for tips on how to find this stuff out – noting that a key method is to talk to past students. (Ask the course coordinator for referrals and if they won't give them, ask yourself, if not them, why not.)

4. What **business models** are there? Which work best and why?

In the UK, the main business models are sole trader, partnership, limited liability partnership, limited liability company and franchise. Don't panic if this is new to you – we'll get into this more a bit later. We just wanted to point out that this is another decision you need to make when you're figuring out the way your business is going to look.

The advantages and disadvantages are going to depend on the business you want to set up, level of investment you've got put in, tax stuff and so on. Most of us find this kind of thing deadly dull, but since getting it right can save you thousands and getting it wrong can cost you your house, your marriage and your liberty, it's worth spending a bit of time on. Speak to your accountant or financial adviser and for heaven's sake don't rely on what your very confident mate tells you (unless your very confident mate is an accountant or financial adviser and is stone cold sober at the time). Free advice is worth what you pay for it.

5. What **industry publications** should you be reading?

Find them through talking to people and hitting the Internet. Virtually every industry has newsletters and magazines that tell you more about it. Invest some money in subscribing. Not all publications are worth the subscription cost and your time to read – but you can often get a couple of issues free to see if they will be any good for your purposes, or buy single issues to begin with.

And think laterally. If you're going to be a management consultant for the printing industry, you'll need to know about printing (and direct mail and marketing, probably) *and* about being a management consultant. That's four industries right there.

Subscribe to lots of free e-newsletters – industry, your competitors, related fields, news, government – and regularly check relevant blogs and websites. All this info helps your brain grow.

6. How do you tell what makes a **good investment**? If you're looking at buying into an existing franchise or business, there's more work you need to do.

You must:

- **Read widely** about options for franchising and licensing. Start with government websites, legal info, general advice. Google 'buy franchise' and follow links and sites. Don't get too hooked into any one particular approach (some websites just want to sell you something); but browse and browse and let ideas soak in.

- **Check competitors.** For just about every franchise, there are competitors who may provide better value/better market positioning for you. So before you fall in love with the idea of Sugar Surprise Donuts, make sure you scrutinise Bagel Delight and Muffins R Us too.

- **Check annual reports** and any financial information you can get your hands on. If you can't get hold of figures, assume they have something to hide.

- **Ask the franchisor for delighted franchisees** they can put you in touch with. If they refuse, assume they have none. (And don't settle for any of that 'privacy' guff they give out; give them your phone number and get them to get the franchisees to call you.) Make a list of all the questions you want answered, and ask as many as you are allowed. Tabulate the results and see what you know now.

Make sure all the info ties back to what you want to do with your life. Sometimes opportunities come up that are wonderful, but are just not for you, or not for you right now. Entrepreneurial opportunities are like buses: red, with lots of seats in them. Hang on, that's not right…oh yeah, you wait ages for one and then four come along at the same time. Jump on the one that's going where you want to go and don't give the others a second thought.

Finding out the stuff you need to know

In the previous bit we covered a lot of ground, about a lot of things you're going to need to know. This bit talks about three ways to find stuff out.

1. Talk to people already doing it

When people talk in their high-falutin' way about 'networking', all they mean is talking to people. You've already done this to find out more about your chosen option and if it will work for you; go back to those same people. (If you haven't talked to them, you should do that too.)

Remember that at some level, anyone who is in this field already is your competitor. If you've got a brilliant and original idea about how yours is going to be much, much better than theirs, shut up about it – don't even hint. Do the listening, not the talking!

- **If you are setting up as a specialist consultant, chat to consultants in other areas. Or, if you need to talk to those in the same field as you,** source people in other cities/countries who won't be targeting the same client base as you.

- If you are planning to become a personal trainer or handyman or gardener, most regions will have room for lots and lots of people doing this job. Chat to someone on the other side of town, so they don't feel you're setting up on their doorstep.

How do you find people doing this job? Ask your friends and family. If your friend Sam has suggested you contact her cousin Charlie, give Charlie a call and say, 'Sam gave me your number and suggested I get in touch – I hope that's OK.'

If you ask around and draw blank stares, search the Internet and the phonebook. If you're cold calling, you need to make sure you're not talking to cowboys. A Google search can reveal a lot and, in a professional industry, if the website has typos or is in yellow writing on a black background or smells wrong in some other way, try someone else. (Oh and by the way, if you don't know what's wrong with typos, or even what typos are, and you don't see what's so wrong with yellow writing on a black background, don't try creating your own website without professional help.)

Make sure you've got one of the partners/directors on the phone and be upfront about what you want, while throwing in a few compliments. We don't recommend pretending to be a customer – you wouldn't want someone wasting your time and neither do they. Try 'I hope you don't mind my getting in contact. I'm just setting up a business a bit like yours, though up here in Leicester, and I wondered if it would be possible to take you for a coffee and see if we have anything in common?' Then talk networking and sharing ideas, or explain that you're researching going into the same field (again, emphasise that due to location or specialisation you will be keeping well away from their client base). And pay for the coffee.

Many people will be surprisingly generous with their time and happy to have a phone chat or coffee. Perhaps this is because they're getting an opportunity to talk about something they love dearly. Perhaps they remember with fondness when they were in your position. Just promise yourself you'll be as generous when it's your turn to be consulted as an expert...

Keep your ears open for people with whom you can form a strategic alliance, swap customers/ideas/license products and so on. It helps to make friends in any business.

Go to trade fairs and industry events – just hang about, collect brochures and cards, be seen and get to know the scene and chat to people. You'll learn a lot, and showing your face is how business opportunities come up. This takes some toughening up and the ability to look busy when in fact it's been hours since you spoke to anyone. If you don't develop that busy look and it's obvious you're bored out of your skull, no one will ever speak to you.

Once you've pinned your expert/bloke in the field down for coffee, here's the killer question. Get ready, because it's quite a doozy. Are you ready? Here goes:

- *How did you ever happen to get started in this business?*

Yep. That's it. Just that. 'How did you ever happen to get started in this business?' Then sit back and watch them go. You'll find that one little question breaks them right open – what they did before, what made them think this would be a good idea, what they love, what they hate, the lot. *Resist every temptation to jump in and start telling them your story* (why on earth would you do that? Do you imagine they're even slightly interested? They're not and it's doing you no good at all. Shut up and listen!).

If they don't happen to go there, also try:

- **What do you like? What do you hate?**
- **What are you good at? What aren't you good at?**
- **What works well? What doesn't work?**
- **Where do you get your customers?**
- **Who do you work with?**
- **What would you change?**

Take notes afterwards (but not at the time: you'll remember it all, believe us) – not of everything they said of course, but the stuff that's useful to you, that helps create shortcuts. Respect any areas where they don't want to share.

And pay for the coffee! Did we say that already? (Yes we did.) Really, pay for the coffee.

And listen! Did we say that already? (Yes we did.) Really, really, *really* listen hard. Say as little as you possibly can and listen. This is so much harder than it sounds, and for blokes in particular (sorry to be sexist, but it's OK because it's Steve writing this bit) – especially blokes who've been 20 years in the corporate world – not interrupting and butting in with their uninvited opinion is absolute agony.

2. Hit the Internet

Google the job or profession or industry you've targeted. Spend hours doing this, following links and seeing where they go. Capture systematically the massive and massively helpful information you dig up about your new field and associated areas.

You won't, of course, find out everything – as you know, often some of the biggest companies/most important players don't have a decent Web presence (strange but true). But you'll know everything that Web browsing can teach you, which is a good start, and your time certainly won't be wasted.

Follow individual names too – if you Google an individual's name, you'll often get references to them in their job and past job. Inevitably you'll run into people, and it will impress them if you're able to mention casually, 'Of course, you used to work at European Brands didn't you?' They'll feel warm and important, which is a great way to start your relationship with anyone.

3. Evaluate your market

The previous two items – talking to people already doing it and hitting the Internet – can tell you what's going on in your industry and with particular businesses and individuals. However, that tells you little about the size of your market and whether it's worth getting into.

This is a tricky subject because it's so very different depending on the nature of the industry you're in. If you're planning to launch a magazine, for example (something Steve knows a fair bit about), you can easily find out how many copies existing titles are selling (by looking up their results on the Audit Bureau of Circulations website) and how much they charge for their advertising (by looking up their rate card on their website). You can talk to newsagents and track down readers, you can interview potential advertisers and journalists active within the market. Piece of cake.

If, however, you're trying to start a book publishing business (something Susannah knows a lot about), things are a lot trickier. There's little agreement about the overall value of the market and none whatsoever about where exactly to draw the line between, say, different sectors of fiction (teens and tweens, young adult and adult fiction). And even if you overcome that barrier, publishing is such a hit and (more commonly) miss business that knowing that the last in the *Harry Potter* series sold 11 million copies on its first day tells you nothing, other than that you wish you'd written it.

However, it is certainly worth opening a file and digging hard to find absolutely every fact you possibly can about your chosen industry. You must become a world-class bore about your subject, capable of clearing a room with a well-timed 'Did you know…?'. After all, a subject is only boring to someone who's not passionate about it, and you must research your topic as if your livelihood depended on it, for a fairly obvious reason.

So, ideally you'd want to know:

- **overall size;**

- **growth/decline pattern – is it shooting up (like online merchandising) or down (like newspapers, magazines)?;**

- **sub-sectors – for example, in publishing, fiction versus reference; or in music, classical versus pop;**

- **average sale price – is it going up (like the value of the average TV over the last ten years) or down (like the value of the average TV over the past couple of years, as the global financial crisis and plasma saturation took hold)?;**

- **gross and net margins – gross margin is the retail price less the wholesale price; net margin is how much, on average, the seller is left** with once all costs have been taken into account. Retailing white goods (TVs, fridges) is a cut-throat business with poor margins, because you can easily be undercut; designing unique, expensive fashion is a cut-throat business with great margins, because no one else has your brand and your designs (not for ten minutes, anyway, until someone in China can copy them);

- the key trends – for example, offshore manufacturing; consolidation of major players; technological developments; compliance and legislative developments;

- the key players/your competitors and what is known about them – for example, size, reputation, key personnel, company history, what they are famous for and what they're not good at;

- the key products – are they the same products everyone has been selling for years, or are things changing? Is there room for innovation? Will yours be better that everyone else's, or the same but with better service or more local? (If it's the same product as everyone else's, with no market advantage at all, close this book, put it down and walk away slowly.);

- and then there's…everything else – hard facts, of any kind at all, about your market.

The more you know, the better. The sticking it all together into one big picture of what's going on will help you answer one big question: is this a market you want to get into?

CHAPTER NINE

BUILDING YOUR DREAM TEAM

No man is an island. John Donne said that, quite a long time ago[9], and almost certainly what he had in mind was **you and your new business**. What he meant was that you can't do this alone – and you shouldn't try.

We think you need three people around you: your life partner (John Donne might have called this person a 'wife,' but that was then and this is now and you know who we mean); your mentor, and your specialist adviser (and who knows what John Donne would have called *them*). Actually you don't need to go and *find* a life partner if you don't already have one – it's just that, if you do have such a person in your life, it's vital to have that person on your side. Let's talk about this for a moment, and then we'll talk about your mentor and your specialist adviser.

1) Your life partner

Your circumstances are unique, but it's likely that either you've been given the push from work or you've quit or are about to. Whatever the scenario, the odds are that both you and your significant other will be experiencing exceptionally high levels of stress, which may very well have affected your relationship. There may have been tears, harsh words and quite possibly depression on one or both sides. You have probably had financial worries, and may still have. All of this is bound to put a strain on any relationship and may have exposed areas of weakness in it.

All the more important, then, that you and your partner discuss your next move and agree on it. Ouch, you may say. Don't ask me to talk about it. It's all I have right now, and my partner is not inclined to encourage me to take this risk. True, this is a sensitive and maybe even painful subject. But it's one you just *have* to get under your belt now – or you'll pay for it big time later.

---

[9] Apparently no one told him women are people too.

It's one thing to go out to battle every day, facing difficult odds and making something work when it doesn't look as if you can. It's quite another to do all that – and then come home and face an unsupportive partner or, even worse (much worse, we reckon), the Wall of Silence. It's incredibly tiring and you don't want to experience it. (We should point out, by the way, that neither of us has been exposed to this. We're both of us exceptionally lucky that our lovely partners have been massive supporters of all we've done and have played a great part in our success, such as it's been. But we know enough entrepreneurs who've suffered exactly what we're talking about, and you wouldn't wish it on a dog.)

Make sure you have the support of your family (without it you will not survive – they take the risk with you). Carel Venter, Centre for Synergy Development

Easy enough to say: keep the other half on board. The question, though, is: how, exactly? Well, we wouldn't presume to tell you how to talk your partner round, but since at some stage you obviously have done enough fast talking to get them into bed, you already know how to get them on side. We're not suggesting you use sex as a lure (necessarily), just that you use whatever wily ways work best. Before you launch into 'Honey, I'm going to sell our house and set up as freelance circus trainer', you might want to think about it from their point of view. It's a big leap of trust for them, after all, and no matter how much they love and want to support you, they're probably worrying about whether your business idea will fly, competition, the market, family time, prestige, feeding the kids and losing the house. In other words, they have all the same concerns you do about the whole concept, without the thrill and excitement of actually getting to do what you're doing.

So what works with your dear one? **Honesty goes a long way.** If this is what you've dreamed of doing – if you're so excited about the idea you can hardly breathe – tell them that. They love you and want you to be happy. Being upfront about the risks and possible benefits, how it will work and above all what it means to you, will go a long way.

(Incidentally, it's been our experience that this sort of discussion is always a great relief and afterwards you are likely to feel a massive sense of release. You'll wonder why you were so nervous about it and you'll be excited by what your partner brings in terms of new ideas, encouragement and support.)

Set some time aside for this discussion, by the way – TV and laptops off, kids in bed or otherwise silenced. Give them plenty of opportunity to ask questions and get their head around what you're saying. This is not something to bring up as a new idea while you're running out of the door.

Consider too whether your partner has a role in all this (other than earning money, looking after childcare or making hot dinners while you do your thing). Involving them in your business may or may not be a good idea (see a bit later in the book). Either way, this is the time to see what they think and whether they're interested in getting into the picture.

Another way of getting your significant other on board that can really work is to **treat the question a bit more formally**. Write a detailed business plan (see elsewhere in this book for why this is a good idea anyway), present it to your partner and invite discussion and advice. To do this, you should make it as business-like as possible – it is, after all, a business meeting (and perhaps the first one you'll have had on this new venture). Ideally get someone else to run the meeting, someone who knows you both and whom you both respect. Best of all, it should be a mutual friend rather than a relative. If you wonder why on earth someone would agree to get involved in such a thing, wonder no more. True friends will be keen to help in any way they can and will be flattered to be so highly thought of that you ask them to play this vital role.

Set out the expectations before you get cracking. You may, for example, say that you want to present the plan yourself for 15 minutes or so, and then invite questions at the end. At first you'll both feel a little uncomfortable and may even find it funny (not such a bad thing: it's harder to fight when you're laughing). Remarkably quickly, however, you'll get into it and find that it really does develop into a proper business meeting. The role of your third party is to make sure that you both stick to your expectations and that agreed action points, together with agreed deadlines, are written down. (They should be revisited at the end of the meeting to check that everyone is clear about them, and then distributed afterwards.) You know what? You've just held your first board meeting. And the very last thing you should do is to agree on a date for your second one.

However you do it, getting your partner to agree with what you're doing, understand as much as possible what difference it will bring to your lives and support you, is key to happiness in your home.

2) Your mentor

If you can find an older, more experienced, wise and supportive person to help you think through your business, your chances of succeeding escalate massively. We're not aware of reliable statistics on the subject (do please let us know if you are), so we've made up our own: we reckon it *doubles* your chances of success. We all of us have our blind spots and these will be significant, particularly if we're venturing into new areas. Find someone who balances your inexperience with hard-won expert wisdom; your own natural tendency either to over-optimism or to pessimism, and who acts as a sounding board.

How do you find such a person? You may have someone in your own life already to whom you can turn. Ideally it's someone outside the family, simply because bad things often happen when blood and money mix (see the next section on family and money). Ideally it should be someone who has a little time on their hands – perhaps someone who's had success in their own business ventures and is now retired or semi-retired. They certainly need to be a good listener, with a calm head and an easy manner.

Most important of all, you need to have someone you know you can drop if you choose to, whose sense of themselves is secure enough that if it isn't working for you they won't get all huffy if you take a break for a little while. You really don't want to be stuck with someone with whom you're not getting on, who insists on putting their oar in.

Many business networks and local government bodies can help you find a mentor – there are even grants in some places to supply them free of charge. And that raises another question. Should you pay your mentor? It's not easy to say. On the one hand, you're getting valuable advice and you'll value it more if it's costing you something. On the other hand, you're going to be short enough of the folding stuff as it is. So there's no simple answer to this one. You're lucky if you find the right person, who wants to see you succeed and isn't short of a bob or two, so won't hear of you paying them. If you're lucky enough to find that person, do be very considerate. Respect their time – be on time for meetings and don't postpone them at short notice without an exceptionally good reason. Buy them the occasional thoughtful but not embarrassingly expensive gift as recognition for their help. A written note of appreciation is hugely effective.

A word too on something that may well come up: equity. (Equity simply means ownership of the business. It's usually expressed in percentage terms, so a quarter share of the business would be 25 per cent.) It may arise that your mentor, or other advisers or helpers, gets involved in part-ownership of your venture. That's entirely a matter for you and them, of course. However, there are a couple of things you need to bear in mind. The first is that so-called 'sweat equity', where someone is paid in ownership rather than in cash (or in some combination of both), can have unintended consequences. Suppose your mentor is now a part-owner of your business. Suppose too that there's a choice to be made, a decision about which way to go. Your mentor now isn't an entirely neutral adviser, but instead has an interest in the result. Perhaps this influences his or her advice? It may very well not do any such thing, of course, but at the very least there is now the possibility, and that may start to nag away at you. Do be aware of this.

The second, bigger, issue with equity is another unintended consequence. Suppose you come to an arrangement with someone – let's say your mentor, since that's the context here, giving them 5 per cent equity in your business. At the moment that may not seem a lot, and you even feel embarrassed to talk about 5 per cent of what looks for all the world like bugger all. However, over time that 5 per cent could very well become worth something quite significant. Would you now resent losing 5 per cent of your profits and 5 per cent of your baby? No? Are you sure? Think about it for a little while and you may start to see what we mean...

Paying your mentor makes it a much simpler, cleaner transaction – except that you need to have the cash to do it, and a really good mentor probably won't come cheap. On the other hand, what's the cost of *not* having their advice?

IN PRAISE OF BASTARDS

One of the independent business owners we interviewed for this book, Karen Dickson, told us how important she's found the teachers and mentors in her life. Interestingly, though, she emphasised the value of those who taught her, by example, what kind of leader or business person she chooses *not* to be.

It's a good point: some of your greatest opponents will turn out to be your greatest teachers. 'It is important to see everything in life as an opportunity,' she says. 'Never overlook those who give you a hard time and challenge you. As uncomfortable as it may get, these opponents also provide some of your greatest opportunities for growth.' It's a great perspective, if you can maintain it.

Anyway, now you've sorted out what's in it for them. So what's in it for you? A good mentor provides emotional and psychological support, excellent business acumen, a sounding board and a different perspective, contacts, connections, experience…In fact, it's a pity that the mentor role isn't better appreciated and more widely acknowledged, because it has the potential to turn an ordinary business into a good one and a good one into a great one.

Your adviser/s

> **I have made true friends, not just business acquaintances.** Andy Roy, FInstIB, NeXus Management Solutions

> **Getting with my accountant early to have my financials in order was a huge help. Spending time on a contract in advance was also a big timesaver and worth the investment for a legal contract.** Mary Honan, For Marketing Matters

Another piece of your puzzle is finding a specialist adviser. You may even want, or need, more than one. This character is different from your mentor, whom we might describe as non-executive and whose role is precisely *not* to be involved in the detail of the business that all too often prevents us from seeing the bigger picture.

Your adviser is different, though there is undoubtedly crossover and you may at first not be absolutely clear about where one ends and the other starts. That's OK, because there certainly is overlap. But the distinction is perhaps this: the mentor's contribution is primarily personal and your relationship will be a close and lasting one, whereas the moment you find your adviser is no longer adding value to your business, push them overboard and don't look back. And it's also more likely that your relationship with your personal mentor will be based on friendship and even love (platonic: keep the boundary and never cross it). **Your relationship with your professional adviser, by contrast, could well be warm and personal, but will ultimately be a financial exchange.** You pay your adviser, your adviser gives you value. When that stops being the case, you shake hands, thank them for their help and give them the boot (in the nicest possible way).

Actually we say 'adviser', but in reality there may well be a number of them. Ideally – and this is how Steve operates in his advisory practice – you'll have one 'point person' who sources, introduces, oversees and, eventually, bids farewell to the others.

How do you find a good one? Now we should declare an interest here, because this is what Steve does for a day job. So obviously our first suggestion is, ring Steve (+61 3 9584 4990) or email him at stevecarey@iib.ws. He spends time with a number of businesses of all kinds, working with the owners to develop their potential. And he doesn't mind telling you he loves it. So it's not surprising that we think that the right business adviser – like Steve, for example – can be massively beneficial. The wrong one, by contrast, is worse than an ashtray on a motorbike – and more expensive too.

So, assuming Steve's number is busy or you don't live in Australia, here are five ways to identify a good business adviser:

1. **You like her on first meeting.** This is hugely important and very revealing. A business adviser who can't even build good rapport with you from the get-go is unlikely to be someone you'll be able to get down to hard work with.
2. **She is not fazed by what you tell her**, however unique and overwhelming it seems to you. If she's any good, she'll have seen it all before. Instead she'll have a host of thoughts and advice – only a fraction of which she'll share with you on the first meeting. This is nothing to do with not wanting to give away the good stuff for free, and everything to do with not wanting to overwhelm you with *her* opinions and ideas before she's heard *yours*. So if you find that you can hardly get the issue out before she plunges in with three suggestions as to what you might do, think again. In fact, what you're likely to find is that she says almost – and sometimes, quite literally – nothing at all.
3. **Demonstrable value, fast.** A quick and dirty business plan (and that's the best kind, to begin with), for example, shouldn't take more than a day and should really look and feel like it's uniquely designed for *your*

business, rather than being a template with your details inserted. Nothing wrong with a template, of course: why reinvent the wheel? But the guts of it has to be absolutely your business and no one else's. And it should dramatically sharpen how you see the business too. If it doesn't do all that and more, don't hesitate: *boot her out.* If she can't at least execute a business plan in a flying start, she can't help you.

4. **She has a great network.** We reckon that any good business adviser will have built up a first class network of specialists – IT, HR, OHS...the whole alphabet soup. If she tries to do everything for you herself, *boot her out.* You don't want a jack of all trades. No one can master everything.

5. **She doesn't agree with you all the time.** You really don't want a yes woman helping you out. What you need is someone who challenges your assumptions, throws in lots of valuable ideas, comes up with new thinking. If she doesn't do that, *boot her out.*

You'll have noticed the phrase *boot her out* a fair bit up there. You need to be decisive. It rarely, if ever, gets better with a business adviser. Give her a couple of months, perhaps, and if she's not wowing you, *boot her out.* There are plenty more out there, and it is after all an unregulated industry. Any fool can call themselves a business adviser – including failed business people.

And you'll notice that we don't suggest taking up references as a way of finding a good 'un. Our experience is that anyone who's been at it for even a short while can always rustle up some impressive-sounding testimonials, and they don't guarantee the quality of the person at all. Put it this way: if someone asks *you* to recommend them, would you? You probably would, if it meant getting rid of them and avoiding the embarrassment of telling them you wouldn't use them again if they were the last person on earth. It's the same thing with their job history. It doesn't matter if they really, truly were the CEO of a huge company – it might have been for about ten minutes and they might be the one who sent that company bankrupt and anyway maybe they were good as a CEO but pants as a business adviser. So don't be impressed by impressive-sounding job titles. While a person's work history and references can help you sort the wheat from the chaff, you still need to treat them with a fair deal of scepticism and focus on how they can help you.

A lot of small businesses don't have a business adviser. A lot manage without. A lot fail. We think they're as essential as all the other advisers and helpers we're about to talk about. But a bad one is worse than none at all.

A lot of the stuff above about finding the right person and figuring out if they are in fact the right person applies to every type of adviser.

Right, who else?

Your **accountant** knows two important things: your financials and what they mean. That's a big help and a smart accountant can be a great boon. If you don't have one, or yours is a bit ordinary, ask around until you find a smart one. If that doesn't work, meet a few until you find one on the right wavelength.

Our experience is that accountants, typically, are not good strategic or forward thinkers – after all, by training and habit they are mostly concerned with reconciling what's already happened rather than forging a path into the future. So if you fancy your accountant in this role, just be aware of this. Of course, some are excellent and show it in having built thriving and successful businesses of their own.

CASE STUDY

Interview: Paul Rattenbury, business consultant

Paul spent 30 years rising through the ranks with a major UK department store chain, moving 18 times and clocking up millions of air miles in the process, before his position was made redundant in 2002. Since then he has been involved at senior level in a retail chain start-up (which went bust) and straightening out a pharmacy retail chain acquisition. He is now a business consultant, selling his skills and expertise to retail and other clients.

'Of course you get comfortable in the corporate world – the big final salary pension that you're not contributing to, the bonuses, the company car and all that. Even so, it only took me a very short while to go through the grief cycle when my position was made redundant in

2002: I recovered very quickly. I certainly didn't miss the travel, for one thing – I did 40,000 miles in my last year, for example.

'I'd worked with business consultants myself, when I was with Debenhams, and thought of them as in one of two categories: the hole-pluggers, who'd come in to fill gaps, and the high level, expensive ones who came and produced thick analytical reports. I didn't want to do either of those things – I wanted to be somewhere in between, I guess, someone who could use their skill and experience to help smaller retail businesses develop some of the systems and smart thinking of the big chains.

'What advice would I offer someone wishing to set up as a business consultant? Three main things, I think:

1. **Be prepared and be realistic.** If you're going in cold, you're going to need time to learn your game and you need to be able to afford to do so. I'd say you need a year or two at least – it's a slow burn – and if you need to be earning serious money right away it's probably not for you. Be realistic too about how easy it's going to be: be prepared to get knocked back a fair bit, especially at the beginning.

2. Related to that, **don't expect the corporate ride**. It was quite a shock for me after 30 years to suddenly have to buy my own car and pay for my own petrol, for example. It's little things like that you perhaps get a bit too used to in the corporate world. When you have your own business, if you need to book travel, you book it yourself, that kind of thing. Actually there is a flip side to this, in that you find more of your skills and experience actually get used in small business than in the corporate environment. There, if you need sales training you usually end up getting someone to do it for you, whereas with independent businesses you do it for them. That I love, I must say – it's such fun to be so heavily hands on!

3. **Know your product!** You really must know what it is you're offering. Experience by itself isn't a product, at least not in a way that your clients will recognise. After a year I'm getting clearer about what it is

I'm offering, which is around the areas of operational management and change management, though of course you don't necessarily use those corporate terms around smaller businesses.

'And what do I think makes the difference between an independent business owner and someone who succeeds in the corporate world? I think it's around the areas of self-confidence and brashness, and not wanting to do what you're told. Think of Alan Sugar, for example: can you imagine him being a good employee? Absolutely not. No bugger's going to tell Alan Sugar how to do things. And in the classical, education-system way you couldn't call him 'well educated' either. But of course he's sharper than a box of knives. After all, the heart of business isn't all that hard when it comes down to it: you make or buy a product and you sell it.

'Would I go back into the corporate world? Actually, I would. I have been asked lots of times and I've always said no, but that's because what I won't do is go backwards – I've been there, done that. So for me it would need to be a start-up if I was going to do it, because that's new and exciting. I want to keep moving, I crave action and excitement and new things. The thought of retiring fills me with dread!'

Your **lawyer** is your guardian! He or she makes sure you're doing it all right. Especially if you are setting up any kind of complex structure for your business, or if your product or service has possible risks or liabilities, your lawyer makes sure everything is covered. In our experience, a lawyer is even less likely to be a good strategic thinker and even more likely to be risk-averse than your accountant. That's what you want. Think of this person as providing balance to your own appetite for risk (and as an entrepreneur you're bound to be a risk-taker).

A **human resources consultant** is a splendid idea if you're taking on staff, especially if you've never hired or managed people before. He or she can advise on structure, pay rates, conditions, legalities, as well as helping you find the right people. Above all, they'll give you a framework for setting expectations – in other words, an employment contract that states formally what you want from staff and what you'll give them in return.

Marketing: one of the things said about small business is that you need to be a marketing expert, along with a sales expert, product expert, manager, accountant and so on. As you can see from this chapter, we don't believe this. You need to know where you're going and have the commitment, but beyond that, there are lots of very specific skills out there and it's a good idea to respect them. Being able to use Excel doesn't make you an accountant. Being able to send an email doesn't make you an IT specialist. Being able to put an ad in the local paper doesn't make you a marketing specialist.

Right, lecture over. Why marketing? It's the bit that brings you the customers, who give you money, so ultimately the bit that makes your business work (or not). So it's really important. Unfortunately, it's also the bit that lots of people assume they can do for themselves. Read Chapter 11 and you can be one of them! (Just kidding.) Like anything else, some people have a flair for understanding customers, products and markets; figuring out how to reach them and putting super promotions together, which often means writing copy, creating ads and brochures and websites. If you are one of them, that's great. If you're not, if at all possible get someone in to do it properly. Marketing is the window through which the outside world sees you – you want it to be superb.

Oh, in this department, you'll probably need a **designer** to sort you out a logo or whatnot. You can often get something really snappy from a student on the cheap, or someone's employee doing work on the side. Unless you've got money to burn, don't go to a design and branding consultant.

IT is the same as marketing really – either you can do it or you can't – and if you can't, don't try. You'll probably want a website, for a start, and you'll need branded email (so you can be Jackie@yourbusinessname.co.uk rather than Jackie73@talktalk.net) and fast, reliable broadband and servers and automatic backup and, and, and…all that good stuff. You could probably do it for yourself, if you really tried. Don't. Instead, find a good expert and get them to do it for you. You don't have time to learn through your mistakes, which is what'll happen.

These people are not your employees, by the way; they are working for you on contract, from their office or their home or maybe in your office one day a week. They are running their own small business. They're on your side – and if they're not, *boot them out* and find someone better.

Why aren't they employees then? What about staff?

We read every single book ever written about starting businesses before writing this one (that's right, all 2,756,937 of them). And boy, do some of the books out there make some big, fat assumptions.

Have you got some of those books on your bedside table? Not keeping company with us, we hope? In fact, do us a favour. If you have a book that states that you need to begin with at least five staff – like a receptionist, sales person, accountant and a couple of other bodies who we forget because that book annoyed us so much we chucked it out – chuck it out.

Know this: *you don't necessarily need to hire staff.* You can, of course you can – who are we to tell you that you can't – but you don't *need* to.

We always say about employees what we always say about absolutely any business cost: if you don't need them, don't have them. Taking on people is seriously hard work, what with recruiting, paperwork, training, paperwork, healthy and safety, paperwork, pension schemes and paperwork. And then there's the whole management aspect of it, which is certain to give you a new-found understanding (if not respect) for the difficulties your old boss had trying to manage you. She might have been lousy at it, but as you'll soon find out if you try it for yourself, there's a lot to be lousy at.

The Yellow Pages is full of people – working for themselves, just like you and us – who would love to come and do your books for half a day a fortnight or whatever you need. You don't need more of their time than this and you certainly don't need to become their employer.

But it all depends on the business you're setting up, of course, and only you know if you do need more people. **If there are job functions you just can't do or if you find yourself consistently refusing work** and so incredibly busy you don't get to go to the toilet until afternoon tea time, then staff may be a good idea.

So if you want to bring people in, how to go about it?

Anyone can run an ad in the paper…but if you've not done this before, it might be wise to get some help from an HR consultant on how to write the ad, which paper or website to run it in, interviewing techniques, remuneration and legals. Business Link can also help you out on this, if you've not got the cash to hire in someone (though if you've not got the cash to hire an HR consultant for a few hours, you almost certainly don't have the cash to hire staff). At the very least, contact one and have a chat about it: she won't have the meter running until you book her, and you'll get a sense for what she does and what you need to bear in mind.

Don't forget the most important thing: yours is a small business and you'll probably spend a lot of time in it, so make sure any employees are people who aren't just great at the job but whom you enjoy spending time with too.

And finally, in your dream team:

You: don't forget you. And here's a secret – the absolute number one reason small businesses succeed or fail is…you. On the one hand, there is the entrepreneur who knows her strengths and her limits, and sticks to one and outsources solutions to the other. On the other, there is the entrepreneur who tries to do everything and does none of it well. So when you're figuring out every else's place in your business, think about your own too. Yes, of course, at first you may well have to be jack-of-all-trades. But once you get going and you can add in help here and support there, what role do you want to play? Do you want to be general manager and hire in everyone else? Or sales director and have other people doing the numbers and the promotions? Or is production your thing, so you'll bring in sales and marketing people?

We're not going to tell you what to do (we're kidding of course: we *are* going to tell you what to do, otherwise you've just wasted a tenner), but this is a good time to **think about your own strengths and weaknesses**, what role you will enjoy the most (that's the point), what role you might do best at (hopefully similar) and have a vague plan about who will do the other bits. You can't do it all. Really and truly.

If you can assemble all these people before you start – fabulous. If you find them and build on your team as you go along – also fabulous, as the further in you are, the more you will know about what you need and what sort of person you are looking for. (Except for you – you need to be there from the start.) And pick and choose who you need. You probably don't need/don't want/can't afford everyone we've listed above. Steve and Susannah started their business with an accountant who writes monosyllabic emails (but is excellent at minimising tax); Susannah's brother as IT guy, and Susannah's partner to do the logo. That was it. We did OK and added the other bits as we went along.

Right at the beginning, have a formal board meeting with your mentor, your business adviser and anyone else pivotal, at which major strategic and tactical issues are thrashed out – and abide by the decisions. You may well decide to keep the veto yourself, and make it clear to everyone that the final word and final decision will be yours. Or you may be brave enough to take the majority decision. Either way is fine, so long as you decide in advance which way you're going and make it clear (in writing). You really can't start off saying you'll go with the majority and then change your mind as soon as you don't like the decision.

Do the board meeting thing again a month later, and a month after that. In fact, keep doing it. It's a great way of taking time out to ensure you're going in the right direction, to build and fulfil action points and to look back at how far you've come.

So there you have it. You now have a dream team, and have just dramatically increased your chances of making this work. You're on your way!

CHAPTER TEN

TAKE YOUR PARTNERS

I wish I'd understood the impact of WORKING WITH someone...so many people try to SELL TO their clients, and it is so much more powerful to form a partnership. Alison Richardson, Richardson Associates

1. Two heads are better than one

So here you are, surrounded by help. But who's at the helm? Should you be running the ship on your own or **would it be better to go into business with someone?**

In reality it's unlikely that you'll be answering this question in the abstract, because either you'll have a partner in mind as you come up with the idea for your business or the opportunity to buy someone else's; or you won't. It's less common that you'll go off looking for a partner, unless that partner is primarily there to provide funding. However, you may have a potential partner and not be certain as to whether it's a good idea to go into partnership or not.

We'll talk in this bit as if you're choosing one business partner; of course you could team up with two or more others. However many people there are round the table, the key thing is to make sure the dynamic is going to be right. You don't want to be hurling staplers as soon as the going gets tough; it wouldn't be nice to have some of you ganging up on the others when crunch time happens.

We know what we're talking about intimately: Susannah and Steve have been working together for a few years now and in all that time we've never fallen out or even had a proper row. Quite sickening, really. Of course we've disagreed about things, and in many ways we have very different perspectives on things. But that's one of the best reasons for working together in the first place, because complementary ways of looking at the world are what enable you to see more than you would otherwise. Two heads are better than one, and all that malarkey. The secret to our success? We were friends first, so that helped – we knew we'd like hanging out together. We admire and respect each other's strengths and recognise that we have things we're both good at (writing and arguing); things one of us is good at (detail) and stuff the other is an expert at (avoiding detail). We're a good team, and if you can find someone you can work with as well as we do, you'll be in a lucky position to take on the world.

Having a business partner helps you tackle some of the least fun things about running a small business:

- **You've got a buddy!** It can be a lonely old slog, running your own show – just you every day, thumping away at the computer, chasing the business. No one to bounce ideas off; no one to have a G&T with on a summer afternoon. Your partner or friends will make sympathetic noises, but having a business partner means you have someone who really knows what's going on and can work with you, celebrate with you, commiserate with you.

- **Double the number of people** on the job. Twice the number of people making calls; twice the number of people networking. If you're out with flu, there's still someone to answer the phone. Double the skills base, too; either more experience in one area, or a wider range of experience.

So a business partner can benefit your business and make your day to day much more fun.

The trickiest bit is finding the right person really – all that like/trust/respect thing we said above. Unfortunately, it's not often that someone with a complementary match of skills who is also looking to quit their job wanders along at just the right moment. It can happen (it did for us), but if it doesn't, don't despair. What's actually more likely, as you circulate more and more in Entrepreneur World, is that you'll meet Mr or Ms Right as you go along and decide to team up in one of your existing ventures, or in something new altogether. Which is a great outcome.

But partnerships can and do go wrong, and perhaps you've heard or witnessed (or even experienced) horror stories that make you nervous. So let's take a quick look at how a partnership might go wrong, how to ensure it doesn't and, more positively, how to give yourself the best chance of it going spectacularly well.

We reckon a partnership only ever goes wrong for three reasons:

1. You picked the **wrong person**.
2. You picked the right person, but you **didn't make expectations clear**.
3. You picked the right person and you made expectations clear, but **things changed later on and you couldn't adjust**.

So let's deal with these in order.

First and foremost, partnership is only going to work if you **pick the right person**. That, of course, is easier said than done, since really the only way you know you've picked the right person is if it works; and you'll sure as hell know you've picked the wrong person if it fails spectacularly. However, that fine point aside, it would seem to make a lot of sense to pick someone who brings something different from what you already have. In other words, if you're a visionary type, it's likely you'll be crap at paperwork and detail. Conversely, if you're a highly effective implementer, it is probable (though not certain) that you'll not be so great at the big picture stuff. If you're an outgoing, sales-y character who is always on the phone and out to meetings setting up deals, then it's probable, though again not certain, that you'll regard paperwork as a necessary evil (and, frankly, you're not even convinced it's necessary). That means you need someone who's got your back.

If you know your own type, it's then not hard to see where the gaps might be. The trouble is, many of us find ourselves in roles with very blurry edges, so that we end up doing some stuff we're not really crazy about as part of the overall package. (Incidentally, it's our considered opinion that many people are unhappy and/or unsuccessful at work not because they're no good, but just because they're trying very hard to do something at which they'll never be great. Find out what your passion is and it's amazing how happy and successful you'll be, and how easy it all feels.)

If you *don't* know your own type, we'd recommend you spend a little time working it out. Do a personality profile, such as Myers-Briggs or DISC or the

Enneagram or any of the others: they all have different slants and approaches, but they all help you to understand yourself and your behaviours better.

So the fundamental principle here is simply this: **team up with someone who adds value** (and to whom you add value, of course).

Oh, and on the topic of picking the right person, you want it to be someone you **like, respect** and **trust**. Like, because really, you don't want to spend a lot of time with someone you don't like. Respect, because the two of you will (hopefully) be talking through business decisions together and you want to be doing that with someone whose opinion you value. Trust, because if you set up a business together, you need to know the other person won't run off with the joint assets and leave you liable for all kinds of nasties.

If you're not close to 100 per cent sure about all these things, a strategic partnership between separate businesses might well be a better option (read on).

The second way to make sure this goes well, as we said above, is to **make sure that you and your working partner have clarity on what's expected of you both**. It is all too easy to roll up your sleeves and rush in, flailing away at the tasks you face without being at all clear what you hope to achieve and how you intend to achieve it. Stop. Make a plan and get yourself and your business partner to make very clear to each other exactly how you intend to take on the task in hand, how you're going to measure it and when you are going to pause and take stock. An ounce of prevention is worth a pound of cure, and agreeing your plan in advance is certainly time well spent.

Assuming you've picked your partner well and have been clear with each other about how this is all going to work, then logically the only way things *won't* work out is when these agreed expectations are based on a situation that changes and to which you cannot satisfactorily adapt yourselves. If, for example, you're in business together and your business partner is headhunted for a dream job that pays five times what you both believe it's possible to earn in the venture you're working on, then it's unlikely that the partnership is going to survive. All you can do is to wish your partner well and shake hands.

Or perhaps the business really doesn't deliver what you had hoped. That, too, is a change of circumstance not covered in your original set of expectations.

And then there is the less clear-cut situation, when you've picked each other well and been clear about your expectations, and simply find that **one or both of you change along the journey**. It happens. People find other things that excite them, or find or lose religion or a new partner, or get sick… there are any number of things that can occur which change circumstances. If that happens, you just need to accept the change gracefully and part company in the very best way you can manage.

But if you can manage all that, partnership can be a huge winner.

2. Keeping it in the family

For most of human history, and in every culture throughout the world, business has meant family. We talk about a 'mom and pop' business and perhaps we think of a corner shop that gets handed down when the old man and old lady retire. We think about the business operator telling the kids: 'One day, all this will be yours'.

But just because it's history doesn't make it right. After all, we used to torture people because their God had different dietary recommendations from our God. It's bad enough that you don't get to choose your own relations, without having to go into business with them as well. Truly terrible things can happen when you mix blood and money.

What are we saying, that there's no possibility of working happily and productively within a family unit? No, not at all. In fact, when it works well, it's a great way for people related to each other to spend time together and to make each other rich. After all, when you retire, you want your money to go to your family (presumably), and what better way than to hand down the business as well as the cash?

It's just that when it's bad, it's very, very bad indeed. We'll talk here for a little while about the upsides, and then for a fair bit longer about the downsides. If, after all that, you decide to push on with business as usual within the family, then at least you've gone into it forewarned.

(Do we sound embittered or sour, by the way? We certainly don't mean to. Neither of us has ever started or run businesses with relatives, and in the right circumstances we can both think of family members we'd very much enjoy working with. Our feelings about it are based on the horrors we've seen when families and businesses collide. It ain't pretty, believe us.)

So, what's the upside? Well:

- **You get to be with the one you love.** Lot to be said for that. You enjoy each other's company, you just hit it off, you have the same sense of humour, you get a kick out of being together. And yet, for most of us, during the week we only see each other at the very start and the very end of the day. Why does it have to be that way?

- **You keep it in the family.** When you exit the business, it seems a terrible shame not to hand it over to someone close to you. And yet, rather than just handing over cash from the sale of your business, why not hand over the whole thing?

- **You know what you're getting.** You know their strengths and, God knows, you know their funny little ways. Being a known quantity, you can anticipate how they're going to respond to most things.

- **Tradition.** A business is very often intimately connected with the community it serves, so the family and the community often overlap within the business.

- **You have things in common.** Your values and aspirations are likely to align. And if you have to leave early one evening because your kids have a school concert on, you know you're going to get a sympathetic hearing.

- **You share a genetic inheritance.** You know they care deeply about you, and you about them. You may very well complain about each other, but the moment anyone else from outside the family has a crack, you close ranks and defend your own. These are all great qualities to have around a business, so that when the going gets tough you know you can depend on those around you.

Yes, there's a lot to be said for working together as a family. And, as we say, when it works well it is a beautiful thing. Nothing in business can quite match the real and lasting pleasure you get from success that is shared between people who have worked together and then celebrated that sense of achievement together. You've taken on the world together, and won.

So why the warning light? Why are we so keen for you to make sure you know what you're letting yourself in for? Well, as we've said before, terrible things can happen when you mix blood and money.

For one thing, many people find it's a terrible shock when they try and work together with someone they love. Suddenly that funny way they have of sniffing all the time can become the most infuriating thing in the entire world. All those little endearing habits aren't so endearing any more.

Besides, we **each of us have different personas** we adopt in different circumstances. Perhaps at home we're quiet, reserved types who like to observe the fireworks but don't get too excited about stuff; and then at work we need to take charge and make sure that things get done on time and to a high standard. Or maybe it's the opposite and we need to be diplomats and charmsters with our customers, which really isn't the way we are at home. Whatever the differences, it's likely that you behave in certain ways at home and quite differently at work.

Secondly, you can **multiply the results** of that changed dynamic when you're talking about relationships. If you're a husband and wife team who get along perfectly well at home, are you sure that won't be different at work? It's easier to run a home as a team, with no one in charge, than it is a business, where sometimes tough decisions have to be taken and you can't always agree.

And then there's money. Money changes everything – the absence of it, the prospect of it, the having of it. It is like water, in that it finds cracks. If you have different values or different views of the world (and you almost certainly do), then it will dramatise and highlight those differences in ways you may never have imagined.

Fourthly and finally, there's the potential for **confusion between entitlement and earnings**. If you are two sisters, for example, and you build a business together that goes well, how should the spoils be divided up? Should it be 50–50, on the basis that this was an equal partnership between siblings? Or perhaps it was Sister A's idea and frankly Sister B hasn't worked nearly as hard at it as she has. But maybe Sister B is the smart one, who has added massive value to the business, despite having most of her best ideas during the school run. And maybe she has five kids and no partner, so her financial needs are greater than Sister A, who's single and already has a pot of money anyway. But then maybe Sister B wants to leave and Sister A wants to stay. What now?

Or suppose that there are three children in the business and one of them wants to go off and do his own thing. Does he still get a third of the business? Really? Even though he hasn't been around for the past decade slaving away when the others have? But on the other hand he is just as much entitled to a share of the inheritance as the others, regardless of all that, isn't he?

And, while we're looking at things that can go awry, there is the difficulty of the parental role. In the traditional model, and certainly that of the ageing generation, this is often the father; he sees himself as the family bread-winner, the man of the house, the one on whom everyone depends to hold things together. So it is in the business, too: he built it up, he worked so hard for so many years. Then the time comes for him to start thinking about life after the business – in itself a challenging and unwelcome thought, for it brings up intimations of mortality and the certainty of death…hardly a cheery thought for even the most sanguine of characters (which he is not).

So he decides to hand over the business to the adult child. And guess what? The adult child isn't keen or isn't capable or has a different spin on where the business should go, which means that father gets disappointed and starts to feel that he isn't appreciated or understood or loved, or something. The potential for moral or even financial blackmail isn't very far away. Or perhaps the adult child *is* capable, but in reality 'handing over' actually means an erratic and inconsistent set of behaviours from the old man that means he gives up just enough that the business can develop a serious wobble, but not enough that his son can actually take control of the wheel and get it back on track. And that, of course, confirms in the old man's mind what he always knew – that he and only he knew how to run the place, so perhaps it'd be better for all concerned if he just rolled his sleeves up and made sure everything was OK again. (Not that he actually tells anyone that's what he's doing. He just barges back in and pulls back all the responsibility he half-handed over.)

That's one ugly scenario and it gets played out many, many times. Has Rupert Murdoch sorted out his kids and who's getting what yet? We kind of lost track a few years ago, as, we suspect, did he. A friend of Susannah's is going through this right now (not on a Murdoch scale) with a small family business that's been running for 20 years: now the parents are retiring, the adult son is changing the business direction and the parents don't like it, and no one is talking to anyone else. Is any business worth the loss of a relationship with people you love?

And then there's the husband and wife team. Let's say, just because it's a common scenario, that he's been made redundant and decides to start his own business, and that she's a trained bookkeeper and/or accountant, so they agree that she'll look after the numbers. Fast forward three or four years and you have a nice business, going well. So far it's been exciting and a real rollercoaster – winning those first incredible contracts, getting premises, expanding, discovering that it really was a good idea in the first place…what larks!

And then reality sets in. Perhaps he continues to have fun, getting out there and winning the contracts, working hard but getting the glory, while she finds that a bigger business means more work and perhaps more than she's really comfortable with. Plus, in ways she hadn't expected, her role seems to have expanded to take in all the crap jobs – answering the phones, organising the office, hiring and firing (when did sacking people become *her* responsibility? Especially when he takes the decisions!) and so on and on and on… The business can't really afford to replace her with all the specialists it would take to do what she's been doing, and besides as an employee of the business she's bringing home money that the household relies on. And before she knows it, the rollercoaster's slowed down and become a treadmill and excitement becomes resentment.

These are just a couple of the many, many scenarios that can unfold and that have one thing in common – the presence of family issues overlaying, or underpinning, the performance and execution of the business. We're sure that, given about five seconds or so, you can come up with other similarly nightmarish scenarios, and perhaps even ones in which you can imagine yourself. If that is the case, then that's terrific, because it means this chapter has done its job: to point out to you some of the potential pitfalls of keeping it in the family. Having thought it through, you may well decide to proceed anyway and that's absolutely fine: you'll be doing so with the knowledge of what you need to be careful about. That's no bad thing at all.

3. The strategic alliance

So far in this section we've talked about keeping it in the family (fraught with danger) and starting up in business with a partner (difficulty rating not so high). Now we'd like to cover off a relationship that is based more on business connections and opportunities, rather than being a familial or relationship-based one.

What follows is a number of scenarios that should help you think about your own business in such a way that your potential strategic partners should begin to materialise from the fog, ideally waving their arms around above their heads and shouting, 'Here! I'm over here! Hey, don't forget me!'

Why try and do it all by yourself? After all, if you yourself have a supplier you trust and who does great work and that person recommends someone else to you, don't you automatically assume that this new person must be pretty good? If you had to choose between someone you'd never heard of and someone who came recommended, wouldn't you choose the latter?

In what follows, it helps to make this assumption: *in your area (either geographically or niche-wise) are between five and 50 businesses that could be the perfect strategic partners for you*. Now, knowing that they exist, you have some questions to ask yourself (and answer): who are they? Where are they? How do I make contact?

If, for example, you're launching a **Web design** business, then maybe you want to team up with a **Web strategist** and/or perhaps a **website copy-writer**. If you're launching a **graphic design** business, again it makes sense to turn up at meetings accompanied by someone who can write the copy. That way, you can offer a complete solution and work with someone to provide it. **Graphic designers** and **Web designers** can work together as often clients need both, and most people specialise in one and not the other.

If yours is a **bookkeeping** business, looking after the figures for a number of organisations, then you'll become aware of other things they need, which you can't help them with directly: sales and marketing expertise, for example, or human resources or recruitment or IT. If you can refer them to someone you work with who covers these needs, then your clients benefit and so too does the person you're so warmly recommending.

If you're an **event planner**, you'd want to develop a roster of suppliers – **caterers, florists, linen, photographers, master of ceremonies**...If you're a **residential architect**, you'd build up a good strategic alliance with local **estate agents**, who would know when a client is looking to demolish and rebuild or even just extend.

This of course makes you yourself valuable as a source of prospects. In return, you can either get a pat on the back or prospects supplied back to you.

If you're a **builder**, maybe you need to develop a strategic relationship with an architect, with an estate agent, with an **electrician**, with **landscape gardeners**, with a **painter and decorator**. All of them will not only do work for you, but should bring work to you.

What about **retail**? If you run a **sporting goods** shop, say, you need to develop strategic relationships with the local sports clubs, particularly junior ones. They have kit that their players must buy, and if they have to source and sell it for themselves they are just ripe for you to come along and take over that terrible burden. After all, they *hate* handling money and buying and selling – though they love the profit. Imagine, instead, that you were sourcing, looking after and selling their sporting uniforms. What would that get you, if not young players coming to your shop in buying mode? They need boots as well as shorts, bats as well as bags: and there they are, in your shop, with their wallets out.

If you run a **musical instrument retail** store, you need to develop strategic relationships with local schools and also with music tutors. They send their students to you: you give them a great deal. Everybody wins.

If you run a **bookshop**, develop a relationship with the **café** next door by swapping money-off or loyalty discount vouchers; a relationship with the local **deli** and **off-licence**, so they provide stuff for your in-shop events and you promote them; and a relationship with the local **nursery** and **primary school**, so they make posters you can put in your window and you sell books to the parents. Give away discount vouchers to the local CD shop and they can do the same for you.

And almost wherever you are, you need to develop strategic relationships with the businesses around you. If there's a **local traders' association**, join it and get well known among those businesses as an active participant. If there isn't, start one. Put a flyer through the doors of the nearest dozen businesses and get them together, so that you're known as a go-getter and your business is known to them for its customer service and active marketing. And when you're getting your flyers printed, don't forget to chat up the local printer, who gets to deal with the printing requirements of all the local businesses and knows who's busy marketing themselves and, like you, getting flyers printed.

There is bound to be a local **Chamber of Commerce** or chapter of **Business Networking International** (www.bni.co.uk) you can join, that will get you cosying up to local businesses who, like you, are looking for strategic partnerships.

Photographers and **frameshops, travel agents** and **old people's homes, pet shops** and **vets, doctors** and **pharmacies, accountants** and **business advisers, banks** and everyone…there's no end to the opportunities for strategic partnerships, except the limits of your imagination.

It's easy to feel alone in this, working at home on the computer, not seeing anyone but the postman and the dog for days on end. But remember, in the very first chapter we talked about the proportion of the economy driven by people working for themselves or running a small business (lots). There are many people out there too just waiting to be invited to team up with you on marketing initiatives, to take on your HR tangle, to work with you on that bit of your business you don't like and aren't very good at. Go find them.

CHAPTER ELEVEN

TO MARKET, TO MARKET

I have been constantly surprised by my ability to get people on board. I guess everything is a selling job but being someone who never considered herself a sales person I have been constantly surprised at my ability to win clients, obtain funding, recruit good people and create strategic alliances. Jo Rhodes-Lewis, Tangible Developments Ltd

Marketing is the soul of your business. If your marketing is right, all else follows.

By marketing, by the way, we're not talking just about making brochures. We're talking about the strategy at the centre of what you are doing and why. What your product/service is and why. Who is going to buy it. How you're going to reach them. Oh, and making brochures.

This chapter is a whistlestop tour of basic marketing ideas. We think marketing is incredibly important for any small business. For some reason, a lot of people who have no background with brand strategy, pricing and promotions think they can do marketing (in a way that they don't, usually, about accounting or legal advice); yet it's no less technical or important. So if the ideas we talk about here don't sound familiar, we suggest you either do a lot more reading or get yourself a good consultant, or both.

Your brand

Your brand is more than your logo. It's what people (customers and prospects) think of your company; the images and values they associate with you.

Some companies represent their brand through logos, mission statements, straplines – on stationery and collateral such as websites and promotions, on staff uniforms and cars and signage. All of the way things look – colours and fonts and a logo – are designed to bring your business to mind when a potential customer sees something that's part of your company.

Whatever you decide your brand should be, it's best if you roll it out consistently. We worked with a small company who had two or three versions of their company mission statement, depending on where you looked, and three or four different versions of their logo. Yikes! The more consistent you can be, the more luck you'll have getting your brand to mean something.

Think of really famous brands – golden arches, that brown fizzy drink that rots your teeth, the football club with the red shirt. You won't have anything near their spending power on advertising, of course, but in your own niche, you're aiming to be just as recognisable for who you are and what you stand for. It's a question of being famous for what you want to be famous for.

So, what *do* you want to be famous for?

Finding your Unique Selling Point

What's your USP? What's your market niche? What do you do that's different? Why should customers come to you, rather than go to that bloke down the road?

This is going to vary wildly depending on your background. If you make soap penguins, that's nice and clear (though you'll have a bit of fun when you get to the section about finding your market). Try it as a mission statement:

We sell more soap penguins in Europe than anyone else!

If what you do is much more vague, or you're not quite sure how to present it, it's time to narrow it down. A service is often quite difficult to describe because you're not packing up a tangible product, and it's much easier to flex and adapt your offering depending on what suits[10]. This is both good and bad. Obviously, if you're able to be fleet and light footed and adaptive, you've got a huge advantage over bigger companies who are hampered by department structures and paperwork.

On the other hand, it makes it harder for you to figure out exactly what it is you do, and can be a marketing problem. Specialisation (perceived or

---

[10] It's a product, by the way, if it's a thing – soap penguins, doughnuts, boats, pens. It's a service if you can't physically see it, only its results – graphic design, business consulting, gardening.

real) is a good thing from a marketing point of view, so if you're pitching yourself as a jack of all trades, be aware potential customers might see you as a master of none, or they mightn't see you at all.

Be wary of product differentiation by factors that aren't under your control. If you promote your products heavily as 'the only soap penguins made locally in Basingstoke,' and someone else comes and sets up making soap penguins on your doorstep, your customers' perception of you will get all messed up. (That's something to watch out for when you're choosing your business name. 'Basingstoke Soap Penguins Company' may turn out to be a real limitation down the line.)

If you don't know what your USP is now, you need to have it before you start work. It's a fairly hoary old term and some modern types rather look down their noses at it. But we think it still has merit.

Poor USPs:
- **largest (as in we're the largest company);**

- **service oriented (good service is a fine thing to aim for but not a good USP to promote, simply because everyone says it and no one believes it until they've tried you out for themselves. Boasting of 'good service' rarely makes a customer want to choose you above others);**

- **cheapest – see below where we bang on about price.**

(Don't worry, we've got good USPs a bit further down.)

While you're figuring out your USP, factor in what competition is out there and how you will make yourself different. (Whatever field you're going into, there will be competition – don't fall into the trap of thinking otherwise.)

When we set up our publishing consultancy/training business, we checked to see what competition existed. At that time there was no other consultancy/training business in Australia specialising in publishing industry – which wasn't *that* surprising, because publishing is a small industry in Australia. This gave us our market differentiator: 'We're the Australian publishing specialists'.

However:

- **there were consultants who worked across industries and had good reputations in publishing;**

- **there were management consultants/market researchers who worked in publishing, including the 200-pound-gorilla type companies;**

- **there were training companies – lots of them – working in publishing (and some publishing companies actually preferred generalist training companies rather than publishing specialists, on the principle that they didn't want their staff having the same training as their competitors!).**

So although there was no one doing exactly what we decided to do, we still had lots of competition.

- **It's worth noticing, by the way, that we made up for the small size of the industry by offering a wide base of services (consultancy, training and market research). This had the added advantage of spreading the risk and exposing us to more avenues of possible work than would otherwise have been the case. You can always narrow your range of services later, when you get inundated with work (as, thankfully, we have been.) (Sometimes.)**

Think about this, not from your point of view or even from your customers' point of view of you, but from their point of view, full stop. See the world through their eyes. Before you came along, who were they using for the service/product you're offering?

If the answer is no one, is there really is a need for your service/product?

Not having existing competition can be a double-edged sword. It can tell you that there's no call for the service *or* it might be that the need is there but no one else has identified it, and there's a fab wide open space for you. Frankly, this doesn't often happen. There are a lot of people in the world and you have to be pretty clever to come up with a brand new product/service, with plenty of demand, that no one has thought of before. Like that young bloke who made a billion in a couple of years with Facebook, for example. We're not saying it doesn't happen, just that it's a pretty narrow gap you're heading for.

If the answer is, any one of a number of companies, is there really space for your business too?

Having lots of competitors is often seen as bad news, since it's harder to break in. But in fact it can actually be a good thing, as it indicates there's a strong a market that can almost certainly bear another supplier – provided you have something different to offer. It may well be that quite a few of the existing providers *haven't* got themselves a USP, and they'll pretty soon find out why that was such a bad idea.

So in that case the question is, what will you do that's different?

Once you've identified your competition and what they do, figure out what advantages and disadvantages you have in going up against them. These might include:

- **specialisation:** you're the industry expert. This is surprisingly effective. Think about it; if you're looking for a car mechanic and you drive a 2004 VW Golf, wouldn't you be more likely to ring the mechanic advertised as 'the Golf expert' than plain old 'mechanical repairs and services'? If you're worried about narrowing yourself in, remember you can always be the Golf expert on Mondays and Tuesdays and the Honda Civic expert on Wednesdays and Thursdays – it's all about getting your marketing right;

- **geography:** plenty of people doing the same thing in London, but you live in Halifax. Yes, we know we said before that this is a poor USP. It's poor if it's the only thing you can come up with that's different about you, but as part of your mix, it's brilliant;

- **product differences:** yours is longer, faster, deeper, sweeter, stronger, purer or more wicked (all depending on what you're offering);

- **experience/background:** you've got a long list of former clients and specific tasks you've done that impresses prospects;

- **innovative, imaginative:** easy to say, but you do need to prove it! Give examples, otherwise people won't believe you;

- **lack of experience/background:** even an absence can be a virtue. You're a new face on the block with fresh ideas and energy! This can be a harder one to sell, but might work if you have a lot of experience in a field other than the one you're now operating in. It also depends on your area – being a 22-year-old graduate might work in personal training, but probably not in management consulting;

- **size:** you're small, flexible, light on your feet (no overheads means lower cost to your customers compared to the big players). You're smaller, so you work harder. People do like the idea of supporting the little guy (especially if the little guy is cheaper or otherwise better than the big guy);

- **price:** it's a natural instinct when you enter a new market to go hard on price. 'We're going to steal the market away from those other buggers by undercutting them.' And that can sometimes work. But there are problems with this:
  - you'll get customers who are coming to you because you're cheap – i.e. they're cheap too
  - as soon as anyone else undercuts you, these customers will be off like a shot
  - your competitor may well have noticed costs that you're not even aware of yet. There's no point in being cheaper if you're not going to make any profit, is there?
  - good service is expensive to provide and needs to be paid for. It's probably a better idea if your customers pay for it, rather than you – or you won't be around very long to keep on providing it
  - it also devalues your product/service and doesn't do any favours to your industry as a whole ('Soap penguins aren't special – they are really cheap')

THE PRICE IS RIGHT

Don't aim to be cheapest: aim to be best value. Why not be cheapest? Four very good reasons: there's no money in it; there's always someone who can beat you; competing on price favours the big over the small; and customers who really do buy just on price are horrible to deal with and almost by definition have absolutely no loyalty. It's a race to the bottom.

However, that's not to say price shouldn't be an important part of your branding strategy. You might in fact decide to be a premium company – top-end product, glossy brochures reflecting your exclusivity – in which case a premium price matches your image. The beauty of this, of course, is that when you get it right there's a lot of money in it.

In general though, pricing so that you 1. make a good margin and 2. are competitive (within range, whether slightly higher or slightly lower, of any direct competitors) is what you're looking for.

How can you tell?

1.How can you tell if you're making enough money?
Each industry has a range of potential profitability, and some (such as retail) have less than others (such as advertising). You need to know what good profitability in your industry might be. This leads us straight on to…

2.How can you tell what your competitors charge?
Well, you can ask them. Check websites and other public data for a start. If you can't get the info there, get a friend to ring up for a quote. (She wants to sound genuine, but on the other hand not involve them in too much drawing up of detailed costings for her – not fair to waste their time.) Listen to customer feedback too about where you sit in the market, though take it with a pinch of salt or two, since they may well have their own agenda. 'I can get this much cheaper round the corner – will you match their price?' Sure, if they can give you a written quote from round the corner and you want the business badly enough.

On the other hand, if you get consistent feedback from people you trust that your prices are out of sync – too cheap or too expensive – then it's time to do a review.

○ last but not least, who wants to be stingy all their lives? If you're cutting costs to the bone all the time, your place is going to be horrible. Imagine that: no decent toilet-paper, let alone biscuits.

So we strongly recommend you never, ever make price your key selling point.

We're not saying you shouldn't be price competitive of course; but price should never be the only thing you do best. If you feel like disagreeing with us (plenty of people will), go right ahead. But do this through a one-off cheapie intro offer to bring customers in and show them how ace you are, rather than starting your company with the strapline 'We're really cheap'. Unless you're a discount wholesaler, that is, though even then there are other things to emphasise.

Your USP will help you figure out who your customers are and how you will deliver your product – your sales channel, in other words. We'll come to that in a moment. First of all, let's deal with pricing and service – two vital aspects of your marketing, of your business, and of your USP.

A word about service

If you're now thinking you're going to be about average for price and your product isn't that original and you're not planning on being exceptional for service, then you have a problem. You've got to be famous for something, or how will anyone know why they should buy from you and not from someone else? Oh, and don't say 'service' just because your pricing's average – you do actually need to be exceptional, or know how to become so.

'We specialise in quality service'. Good as this sounds in theory, it tends not to work. *Everyone* says their service is good and no one actually believes it until they've tried it out; that first sale is almost always made for some other reason.

The best way to make great service your selling point, of course, is to do it. Don't tell people that you do it, let them discover it for themselves and tell their friends.

Promotions: How will you reach your customers?

Here are our top tips for promotional campaigns:

1. **Look before you leap: test everything**

   To assess any promotional campaign, try and monitor results to see what's working. If something's not working, do something different. Sometimes results may not be clear and you might find yourself going by gut feel – that's OK too.

2. **Consider what kind of results you're looking for**

   Calls? Emails? Direct sales? Referrals from friends? You need to tell people what to do and make it easy for them to do it. And do that before you put your campaign together! And once you're done, check through and make sure all the bits work.

   Susannah recently ran several promotional email campaigns to get customers to request samples for different products. When she checked where the email links were going, she realised the website she was sending customers to made it very hard to ask for sample copies. She replaced the weblink with a 'click here for a sample' button and responses *tripled overnight*.

   And remember that people don't do things unless you ask them to. You can send out the best email in the world, and everyone looks at it and says 'that's nice'. You need to *ask* them to click to your website, or *ask* them to ring you, or *ask* them to tell a friend about you – and then they will.

3. **Know thy customer**

   The most important thing is about promotions is to think about who your target customers are and the best way to reach them. If you're a locally based gardener or personal trainer, advertising in the local paper or a letter box drop in your target area might be the way to go. If you're a specialist legal adviser to boat purchasers, you're going to want to get into that specific community and advertise in boat sales magazines or team up with a boat sales agent.

   How do you figure out the best way to reach your customers (or prospects)? Get into their shoes, that's how. Read the magazines they

FOUR EXAMPLES OF GREAT SERVICE

Last week Steve was walking by a café, outside which sat three customers, each with a dog, at different tables in the sunshine. The owner of the café walked out with three tiny titbits, one for each dog, which she gave them, wordlessly. Cost to the business? Next to nothing. Value? Priceless.

Steve went to buy booze the other day and found he was a few coins short. 'Don't worry about it,' said the guy, 'just give me what you've got.' That little bit of service cost the business next to nothing – but bought a massive amount of customer loyalty and goodwill. No one goes to an off-licence because it advertises 'great service' on the door, but Steve will go back, because that's what he got.

Recently Susannah popped into a bakery with her little boy. After some discussion during which Leo requested baked goods that were inappropriate, in her opinion, for a three year old (vanilla slice, custard tarts, etc), he asked for and received a fruit bun. So the transaction took some time and Susannah was worried the baker would be cranky. Instead, he put the bun in a little bag, handed it to Leo and refused to take money. Will we go back again? Of course. What an inexpensive way to buy repeat business. (Thumbs up to you, Baker's Delight in Brighton!)

What's interesting, by the way, is that it was the actual baker – the bakery owner – who served the greedy three year old, and the franchisee of the booze shop who let Steve off for the change he didn't have. Where owners feel comfortable making such decisions, employees usually don't. There's a tip here: if you end up with staff, let them know it's OK to forego a few pennies in exchange for a customer's lifetime loyalty. It's a case of getting them to understand the bigger game that's going on here.

Something else about great service: if you think back to when you've been really impressed by someone's service, when they've gone the extra mile for you, a lot of the time it's actually when they have stuffed up in the first place and managed to fix it in a really good way. That's worth remembering when you mess your customers around – and it will happen – it's a great chance to be on the ball and apologetic and impress them with your response.

For example, Steve spent some time on the phone trying to get the right person in a big organisation. He rang – went on hold – got cut off – rang again – went on hold – got cut off again. (Sound familiar?) In a fury, he raided the company's website to find a senior contact and banged out a fairly forthright, though constructive, email, pointing out the damage this money-saving lack of service was doing to the business.

Exactly 15 minutes later, his phone rang – a senior manager, with an apology in hand and exactly the information Steve was looking for. He even had the sense to thank Steve for bringing the gap to his attention, so the business could do something about it. Smart.

The result? Impressed by the service, Steve will definitely use the company again – whereas after the fruitless phone calls, he was about to tell people at bus stops that the organisation is rubbish.

When we mess up, or just provide service that's lower than our usual high standards, we make sure we acknowledge and fix asap. We suggest you do same.

Anyway, excellence in what you do is of course integral to running a successful business. But remember that it will help you to keep customers and grow your business, not to start your business in the first place.

read, go to the shows they go to, talk to them as often as you can. The more you understand about them, the better you'll be able to reach them.

This goes for the promotional channels you choose (local paper, as opposed to, say, national TV), your advertising copy, your pictures, the whole lot – target it to the kind of customer you want.

After some years of working for a gardening company, our friend Andrew set up his own company with the wonderfully highbrow byline 'Former Contractor to the Royal Parks, London' – which has strong appeal to potential clients from higher socio-economic backgrounds. To the less posh customers, Andrew phrases it slightly differently: 'I used to trim Diana's bushes'.

Some planning would work here too when thinking about reaching your customers. No matter the size of business you're aiming to set up, you'll need a client database – meaning a way of keeping track of people you work for. This might be something fancy on the computer, or just Excel, or a really big diary or address book – whatever you're comfortable with and can navigate your way around. Think detail here. If you can keep track of clients' partners' names, birthdays, kids, football teams etc and drop them into conversation, they'll love you even more.

4. Make your promotions appropriate to your business

If you're offering cooking parties for children, you might want a cheerful and friendly brochure and website with fun photos. If you are a freelance accountant who travels to people's homes, your collateral is going to want to be more formal and professional. And if your business is at the premium end of the market, a cheap flyer and dodgy website will not do – your collateral represents your business, not the other way around.

5. It's your business – not theirs

Just because someone you know had a lot of success with late-night TV advertising to sell golf clubs does not mean the same promotional strategies will work for you to find accounting clients!

6. Use professionals

This is really an area where you want your stuff smelling top notch. If you're not a designer, we suggest you get someone to create your logo, your stationery, your website. It doesn't have to be a top London agency;

it can be your cousin's friend the university student, as long as he or she is creative and savvy and can find a way to represent you visually. If you're not a marketer, find someone to help you with the copy for your brochures, ads and website. Get everything read through five times – by people with editing qualifications – before you go to print. If your stuff isn't top notch, people won't use you. The best offering in the world, presented badly, will flop.

"What surprised me? 1. The people that you think will refer business to you are the least helpful. 2. How many other companies do not brand themselves – silly approach. 3. My niche is a good one – I am surprised and excited about the opportunities to educate and inform prospects about real, effective, pragmatic marketing." Mary Honan, For Marketing Matters

And these are the promotions we think you might want to try:

- **Business cards**
  Essential if you want to have, you know, customers. We are fans of investing in nice business cards to reflect the quality organisation that they represent, rather than going with a Cheap Print offer. Letterhead and other stationery, on the other hand, is much less key to start with: in many industries you'll find a lot of correspondence is emailed and electronic letterheads used much more. If you're submitting quotes for contracts, though, or anything like that, you'll need the full professional appearance.

- **Website**
  Pretty much your promotional starting point for any company these days. Do think hard about how it fits your business. If you are setting up a local business with a shopfront or a service such as personal training or gardening, a website will be less important than if you're an architect. If you decide you need a website, don't be afraid to spend some money here, if you have it, by getting a company that can work with you on content as well as good design. If you don't have the money, something

CASE STUDY

Interview: Jo Bryant, legal-medical reporting

Jo is an occupational therapist who has been self-employed and has run small businesses from very early in her career.

'After I graduated I had my first job as a community health occupational therapist for the Department of Health. It was good in some ways in that it was flexible, not 9–5, and I had a great manager/mentor. But I come from an entrepreneurial family and couldn't help but see inefficiencies and better ways of doing things everywhere.

'My colleagues weren't bad, it's just that the structure led them to make implausible decisions. Working for a big business, and particularly working for government, is so political – you have to take care not to be seen as uppity and so on.

'So I took myself off to the Centre for Adult Education, where I worked as a lecturer, and combined that with contracting as an occupational therapist for four years. It was there that I experienced the incredible personal satisfaction of reward for effort and innovation: if I had a good day, it was because of my efforts and if I had a shocker, then I only had myself to blame.

'The trouble was, I could not embrace academia. They were nice people, but they seemed to have a lot of meetings, a lot of talk and, it seemed to me, very little action. They had two paces: dead slow and stop. It drove me mad! Even so, I was building good, marketable skills – but there was no opportunity there to focus on them and to exploit them.

'Then in 1981 I had my daughter Amy, after which I did some sessional part-time work and had a few months off. I just knew I didn't want to go back to being an employee. I was doing locums for cash, fell in with a business and used their private rooms.

'But in reality I didn't have a business, I just had a job – I was self-employed! Then when I saw my husband's business and what it might be, I could see what having your own business might mean; employees and doing things properly.

'I saw that I needed accreditation, so I went and got that. And then the second time I set up in business I took it more seriously. I thought I'd been serious before, but this time I knew that I needed to have goals, a plan, but I kind of knew what I was doing. Even so, it wasn't until 2006 that I actually hired my first employee. So, I had been accountable and responsible to myself for earning a full-time income for nearly ten years.

'As I say, I've always been entrepreneurial, open to opportunity, looking for ways to apply my skills where they can add value to a situation. So when a new opportunity presented itself to me, some ten years later, it was literally a phone call out of nowhere one Monday evening. I nearly didn't go, but I was intrigued: what might it turn into? And what it's turned into is this; medico-legal reporting and finally, a growing, thriving business!'

What lessons have I learned?
1. **Develop marketable skills**
2. **Have a 'can do' attitude: find a way, make a way.** That's very important. If you wait until you can see how you can do it, it'll never happen.
3. **And last but not least, if your primary motivation is money, don't do it.** It has to be about the flexibility, the satisfaction – and then, when you get the business right, the money flows as a result. But you can't have that as your first and primary goal, or it just won't work. That's my view, anyway!'

off-the-shelf may well do the trick – just keep it simple and upgrade when you can. If possible, software that enables you to update and change things yourself without going through a Web designer saves lots of time. Also bear in mind that a website is useless without mechanisms for people to find you – which might be search optimisation (good Web designers can do this for you) or a promotional campaign that directs people to you. And once you have your Web address, put it in on all your other collateral!

● **Brochures or flyers**
These are especially good for letterboxing or take-away handouts for personal services. For professional services, a good website might be more appropriate.

● **Advertising**
Consider local papers, radio, industry-specific publications, TV, Google ads, letterboxing, pinning up notices in community locations. As always, picture the people you're trying to reach and how you can best get in contact with them. If in doubt, ask a few clients (or people you'd like to be clients) what they read and where they go to find information, and then try those out.

● **Point of sale material**
This includes working with your retailers to produce posters or other in-store materials to help convince end customers to buy.

● **Viral and social networking campaigns**
Creativity is your only limit. We enjoy marketing campaigns that are honest, funny and a bit different. Good examples change by the minute, so we won't suggest any, but tap 'viral marketing campaign' into your favourite search engine and see what happens.

Don't underestimate what Facebook, MySpace and friends can do. They are immensely popular with a marketing-savvy section of the population, who can sniff out a promotional campaign from 100 miles away. If you want to get into this stuff (known technically as social networking or social engagement), we suggest you hire someone born in the 1990s or later (if you weren't) to assist.

● **Publicity, public relations, launches**

In our experience, people bank on publicity events working much better than they do in real life. Journalists tend to have a million press releases hitting their desks every day, so unless you've got something really outstanding or you're a very well known organisation with a recognisable figurehead who does outlandish things (hi, Richard!) it is difficult to get national publicity. (Though Susannah's brother did once make the national papers by deploying a bloke dressed in a duck suit. That was election time, though, and things often go a bit pear-shaped then.)

Community publicity is a bit more promising, so if you're working in a specialist area or a small community, definitely let your industry magazines/local newspapers know what you're up to.

Public relations – meaning doing good things to build on your branding – is often worthwhile, partly because it's good to do good things and partly because it gives the audience a nice warm feeling when they think of you. So if someone asks for a donation to help a charity, see if you can help them. Go on, do. Oh, and the donation you help them with should never be cash – it should be your product or service – which is less costly for you to provide and reminds your audience of what you do. So if you're a mechanic, offer a free car service as a prize in the raffle. If you make snazzy cupcakes, bake a cake in the shape of a teddy bear for the kids' charity.

● **Giveaways**

Companies with a promotional spend often have pens and other bits of plastic crud implanted with their company name. Does it work? Can't tell you, you'll have to try it. Like anything else, it depends on the market you're targeting. Don't assume instant results; this kind of thing is broad branding, so you may find the recognition and remembrance of your company rises a little among people who received the gift, and that's it (and very successful too). The phone is *not* going to ring off the hook for weeks because you hand out caps with a logo on. It might help you improve your brand recognition, though, or create even more loyal customers. Our general prejudice, we have to tell you, is that spending much on this type of stuff is a mistake. Our absolute conviction is that doing this type of stuff is no substitute for a marketing strategy. (Steve recently met a business that had spent tens of thousands on mousemats and mugs, and not only had little idea what to do with it all, but somehow imagined that they were doing a good marketing job just because they had stacks of this gear. What a waste!)

Promotional companies can help you with these things (not because they're nice but because it's their job). As always, just make sure you know who your targets are and what outcomes you want. Is it better to make 50 high quality leatherette notepad folders, or 3,000 little plastic screen cleaners? Depends who you're trying to reach. Talk to the promotional company you're working with about what it is you're trying to do.

Your sales channel

If you're:

- a business consultant, your customers are small-medium businesses and your sales channel is in person;

- making classy cookies in wedding shapes, your customers are people getting married and wedding caterers, and your sales channel is direct mail order sales through your website;

- a personal trainer, your customers are people living locally who want to get fit, and your sales channel is through the local gym.

We asked lots of people who run their own businesses how they find their customers. Here's what they said worked best:

- referrals and word of mouth
- online/offline networking

WHAT IS NETWORKING?

Networking, networking, networking and another one for free....networking. It is the only way to get business. Dave Boulter, Boulter Associates Pty Ltd

Why would you deprive your friends of the opportunity to do you a favour? Let people around you know what you're up to – whether it be planning, starting out or getting into it.

- **Ask friends if they know anyone who could be a customer.**
- **Go to events where you can meet people – customers, other operators like you, anyone related to your industry…and not related, too.**

Chat to the people next to you at dinner parties about your business. Find out what they do and see if you have any areas of overlap. Go for a drink if you're invited.

Sooner or later, someone will say something like, 'Actually, tell you what, now that you mention it, my cousin is looking for a soap penguin. Why don't I give her your card?' Now if that's an outcome you'd be happy to have, what's wrong with helping the process along a bit? But to get the process started, you have to be willing to tell people what you are doing and how they can help. Without this information, you're not giving them much chance of helping you, are you?

Oh, and carry your business card – at leisure as well as during your working day: you never know when you'll need it.

These two responses were by far the most popular, with 'referrals and word of mouth' getting ten times as many mentions as any other way of getting business. Make that service good! Oh, and ask customers to refer you to their friends – that's the way to get referrals. It's funny that people often don't think to refer you on, but when you ask them to, they suddenly realise they know someone who needs exactly your services.

Other tricks that work for small businesses include:

- **telemarketing/cold calling**
- **public speaking and seminars**
- **local paper advertisements**
- **web advertisements**
- **sub-contracting for other small businesses**
- **leaflet drops around the neighbourhood**
- **your website**
- **writing articles in industry magazines**
- **newsletters, mailshots and other direct marketing**
- **your blog**
- **tendering for contracts**
- **special events for special customers. Tastings, sales, walking tours, social events, networking**

It's going to depend what type of business you are running, of course. A local paper ad is unlikely to work for a specialist business consultant, but is probably absolutely key for a handyman (though the handyman we know swears by dropping leaflets door to door, so go figure). At the end of the day, we recommend that you TEST, TEST, TEST. And if it works, do it again!

Promotional writing

We reckon your business should have a sound, a tone of voice. It should sound like you, of course (this is your business after all), and should probably sound friendly, funny, warm and engaging. Note that while this is probably not true if you're a bookkeeper, it's also the case that, frankly, bookkeepers don't do funny very well anyway. In other words, the type of business you're attracted to should suit your tone of voice, and vice versa.

This 'tone of voice' should be reflected in all your marketing. Avoid the temptation to do the stuffed shirt, which just makes you sound like every other boring business out there. On the other hand, avoid wacky for the sake of it. Nothing is as much of a turn-off as that 'Hey, you don't have to be craaaazeeee to work here, but it helps!!!!' routine.

Actually, shall we tell you what we really think? We honestly believe it's worth getting some help on this stuff. We reckon you can tell a business that's had the help of a good copywriter at some stage, and the interesting thing is that once it's been created, this 'tone of voice' is easy enough to replicate. (Virgin always seem to do jaunty copy well, even down to the small print on their credit cards.)

Regardless of whether you use professional help, here's six of the best – things we reckon work a treat, almost regardless of the type of business you're launching:

- **Testimonials**
  'The finest garden shears I've ever had' – Mrs Emily Bell of Smethwick

- **Evidential claims**
  '85 per cent of our clients come back for more'
  '73 per cent of our customers say these are the finest garden shears they've ever had' (this obviously combines both testimonial and evidential claim in one hit)

- **Guarantees**
  'First time pass or your money back'
  'If you're not happy, bring it back and we'll return your money, no questions asked'
  Note: we don't know why more businesses don't use guarantees. All the evidence (and there's plenty) indicates that customers hardly ever abuse a generous guarantee. And anything at all you can use to reduce FUD (Fear, Uncertainty and Doubt) in the mind of the customer-about-to-be is worth doing, in our book

- **Long copy**
  Works well in a magazine for direct sales (like a letter to customers) or a tube train ad

- **Short copy**
  Works well if people are on the move – newspapers, for example, or billboards
  Note: short copy is harder than long copy, though long copy written well so it doesn't become boring is pretty damned difficult too

Finally, note that whether you use a professional or write stuff yourself, before you send anything off to print or hit the website live button, read it. Then read it again. Then give it to your partner, your mum, your best friend and your aunt, and get them to all read it critically looking for wonky bits like typos, grammatical errors, assumptions, anything that won't sit well with the general public. Then put it to one side for a day or two and do it all again.[11]

How to give good quote

Establish a comprehensive invoice covering all the things you need to say. It's key to bill and charge correctly. Stefan Wasinski, Consulting Well

So you've done your marketing well and your phone is ringing off the hook. Fabulous, darling, absolutely fabulous.

Next: getting the cash in. There is no satisfaction like the satisfaction of collecting your very first cheque. *I* did this, you think: *I* made this happen. And, even better: *I* get to keep it all! It's a wonderful, glowing moment, and many a business owner has her very first cheque framed on the wall as a memento of that special occasion.

What she may well have forgotten, in all the excitement, was the rather embarrassing fact that it cost her three times as much to deliver the end

---

[11] You will almost certainly not have time to do this, but you must do it.

MARKETING ON A SHOESTRING: TEN TOP TIPS

1. A fabulous and funny **email campaign** costs next to nothing – if it gets forwarded on, so much the better.
2. If you're a bit broke, **contra** (swapping) is king: I'll advertise in your magazine and I'll pay you in t-shirts for your staff. You give me a referral to ten top clients and I'll clean your house for a month. And so on…
3. Form a **strategic alliance** with a complementary, non-competing company – work together to share leads and promotional costs.
4. When you've beaten down the other side on price, ask to **pay invoices over a longer period**. This costs them nothing, and unless they are personally responsible for cash flow (which a sales person won't be), they'll do it to get your business.
5. Rope in your friends and family to help with **building a website** (we've done that), **sharing an office** (we've done that), **minding your kids while you work** (we've done that), **print your stationery** (we've done that)…
6. **Network** like billy-ho, at every opportunity and every single day.
7. Get back in touch with your **lapsed customers** – it's much less expensive than creating a new promotional campaign. More effective too.
8. A **letter** is cheaper than a brochure.
9. An **email** is cheaper than a letter.
10. **A phone call** is more expensive than an email, but works far, far better. If you're afraid of the phone, find a way to get over it or it'll cost you, big time.

result as the amount she actually banked. Why? Because she was so keen on getting the job that she overlooked the vital task of working out what she should charge.

It's the old forces of supply and demand. To simplify matters just a little, on the day you launch you have an infinite supply and zero demand. So you're keen – and that's understating it considerably – to get work (and cash) in the door. You want to establish your reputation, get some experience under your belt and customers onto your books and get busy, busy, busy. If you're not careful the result is wild optimism on how fast you think you can complete the task, blended in with absolute paranoia that your client or customer will think you're ripping them off if you charge them anything at all. So you underestimate both how fast you think you can work and how much your client is prepared to pay. You get the gig and you're delighted. Excellent: that's pretty much how it should be. At the start, that is.

As time rolls on and you get busy, your confidence and expertise grow. Finally you start to believe in yourself, while beginning to realise that being BBB (Busy But Broke) is no way to run a business. So your prices go up, as your supply is limited and demand increases. Fast forward perhaps a couple of years and the penny finally drops: you can tell how long this is going to take! You know what people are prepared to pay! Suddenly your quotes become less a stab in the dark and more a matter of science.

There are two methods of costing a job, and only one of them is so obvious you'll certainly have worked it out for yourself: **cost plus**. If a job is going to take you, say, three days and you know what the parts are going to cost, that means that, provided you have worked out a value for your time and labour, you have a good idea of what your costs are. Then you just need to work out what mark-up to add and you're away.

What's that? How much should your mark-up be? Absolutely no idea. Basically you have to do that bit for yourself, working with three variables that are pretty much unique to you: your costs; your industry average and your busy-ness. If you're flat out, your price goes up; if you're desperate for a quid, then it comes down. Yes, we agree this is terrible strategically and price should not, in theory, be fluid like this. But we're realists and our children demand feeding every day, not just when we're up to our necks in work.

The other, less obvious and more interesting, method of quoting is **value-based** charging. Think of it this way: you may put an extremely high value on an hour spent in the company of, say, Brad Pitt. Now if you're the customer and I have an hour of Brad's time available, I know that the value to you is very high and can charge accordingly. If, however, you think he's a dullard, then my charge needs to be adjusted – even though the actual commodity (an hour of Brad Pitt) is exactly the same. It's like the old story about the plumber's bill: a fiver for tapping the pipe and stopping the leak; five hundred quid for knowing where to tap. *That's* value-based charging.

As you'll have worked out by now, because you're smart as a whip, value-based charging is going to get you rich a lot faster than cost plus. And you'll also have recognised that some businesses – plumbing not, in reality, necessarily one of them – lend themselves very well to value-based charging, such as consultancy, financial advice of a high level and prostitution. Others do not, such as plastering, bookkeeping and weeding.

That, in a nutshell, is how to think about quoting. The real secret, to be honest, is not so much how you charge or even what you charge, as how well you conduct yourself. A professional, courteous response that is backed by a good explanation of how the quote has been arrived at, supported by all the evidence that you're going to deliver what you said, when you said and at the price you said, carries far more conviction and is far likelier to get you the gig than a cheaper quote from a fat, leering, smelly scruffbag.

THE LAST WORD ON MARKETING

Do you know the single most important marketing decision you'll make?

It's your business name.

If you've inherited a dreadful business name along with the family business and you can't do anything about it, don't read this bit!

Your business name is on your cards. It's on your website. It's how people find you. It's who you're about to become: 'Jackie, from Flowers Incorporated'; 'Dean, from Hamilton Industries'.

If your business name is memorable and describes your business, you will do much, much better, than if it isn't and it doesn't.

Here are top tips for finding your business name:

1. Memorable is good

'Virgin' is already taken: sorry about that – but you get the point. Puns are fun if you don't mind being a bit cheeky. 'Knobs and Knockers' is a door fittings trader we like. Hairdressers often seem to do a good line in puns – 'Hair Apparent', 'Curl Up and Dye' (in *The Blues Brothers*) etc. If your target audience is a bit more professional, look for words or phrases that ring a bell for your industry or have a link.

We chose our business name, Bloom, because we started out as publishing and communication consultants and wanted something just a bit literary but not too obvious (if you're a Joyce fan like Steve, you can figure this out). We also liked ideas around flowers blooming and business booming – all happy thoughts.

2. Don't go *too* descriptive

This is because you don't want to lock yourself in. If you make a mint as 'Residence Architects' designing residential properties, what happens when you want to get into designing hotels?

3. Aim for easy to spell

'Blue Pavers' is much easier for someone to look up on the Internet than 'Blu Payvas'.

4. Don't go for initials

We really don't like using your initials or your surname for your business. Smith Ltd. MH Marketing Services. Blargh. Boring. Tells us next to nothing about your business. Can't remember it anyway. Lost opportunity. Why be boring and eminently forgettable when you can be interesting and memorable?

You need a bit of a feeling for words to do this bit – either that or a few friends who don't mind you throwing ideas at them.

Once you've got a few top candidates, check if they're already taken or not, which will knock out at least four of your top six options. Then roll them around your mates for feedback.

No business name is perfect, by the way, and you can spend too much time worrying about this. So…find the best you can. And move on!

CHAPTER TWELVE

DOING BUSINESS IN A GLOBAL FINANCIAL CRISIS

In the past, when working for very large corporates at GM or CEO level, heading into a downturn has always been very stressful for me. Today, I'd have to say I've never been more relaxed. Stefan Wasinski, Consulting Well

The worst time was when I experienced a bad debt, the bank withdrew its promise of funding and I made the scary decision to make my entire team redundant and move the business 200 miles away to give it a chance of survival. This required considerable investment from my own funds at a time when I hadn't been paying myself for several months. Making the communication about redundancy and following a very long convoluted process to achieve it nearly sank the business, but I'm happy to say that we came through that and the results have vindicated me. Jo Rhodes-Lewis, Tangible Developments Ltd

These are extraordinary times, and not in a good way. **The economy, if we may be permitted to use a highly technical term, is buggered.** It's no good ignoring it, especially if you're about to head off to start your own business. This chapter looks at what the Global Financial Crisis (GFC) changes, which is everything.

Of course, the very reason you're considering your own start-up may be the GFC itself. The business you were working for may have taken a tumble and you may have been laid off. So you know how tough things can be.

Does this mean your chances of success are diminished? No it doesn't – not if you think your way through what you're doing, look before you leap and choose your target wisely. There are a surprising number of businesses that are extremely resistant to tough times, and quite a few that actually thrive in them.

Before we get into that, though, you need to make sure you're clear on one thing: **the GFC is not going to be the reason you fail.** This is very important, because if you allow yourself to think otherwise, there's the possibility that you'll store it away in the back of your mind and secretly blame it for everything that goes wrong. You must not give headspace to that kind of thinking, because it can become incredibly corrosive.

Steve, in his business advisory practice, has seen many businesses (not his clients, he hastens to add) that, perversely, almost seem to be enjoying the GFC. Suddenly it's not their fault, it's bigger than them. Certainly there are sales people out there who are shrugging their shoulders and wallowing a little. You must not let that happen to you. If you're going into this, go in with your eyes wide open, knowing exactly what you're letting yourself in for.

In addition, you'd have to say that many, if not most, of the businesses that have been hurt by the GFC had problems already. General Motors, Chrysler and, to a lesser extent, Ford have not suddenly found themselves without a market: it had moved away from them years ago. Woolworths didn't just fall in a heap: it had had problems for years.

In fact, there are even those who suggest that the GFC acts a little like a war in thinning out the population and, when the bounce happens, generating a recovery. This is an unpleasant idea and personally we don't think it's worth all the misery it causes. But perhaps there's some truth in it. As Warren Buffet said not so long ago, 'It's only when the tide goes out you can see who's been swimming naked.' There are many, many appallingly run, wasteful businesses that have survived because of the great boom (artificial, as it turns out) we've been through over the past decade or so and are now going out backwards. Well, the tough view is that either they'll smarten up pretty quick and get themselves fit to survive – or they won't make it.

We're not saying, of course, that the GFC doesn't make things tough. It surely does. All we're saying is that by itself it's not responsible for everything that's wrong with business, and it's not an excuse – certainly not for you.

Right, having got that out of our system (and, we hope, into yours), let's take a closer look. Here are three things you need to focus on regarding the GFC:

- **shelter from the storm:** everything that smacks of security, home comfort and hunkering down at home is likely to go well during a recession;

- **downscaling:** maybe people can't afford a big trip to New York and Disneyland, but they can still afford a week at the seaside (and may well feel the need to spend within their own domestic economy). They may not eat out at expensive restaurants so often, but they can still cook up something special at home;

- **uneven impact:** if you're in your mid-20s, living at home and never having experienced a recession or job cuts, you'll be wondering what all the fuss is about. If you're in a recession-proof job, with a tracker mortgage, the world is good. If you're an architect, on the other hand, you may as well be driving a taxi.

Something called the 'Lipstick Index' proposes that certain items sell well in recessionary times – lipstick (obviously), fine chocolates and jewellery are classic examples. However, what's unusual this time round is that consumers are being more capricious: expensive wine, as you might expect, has slid, but we're still loving our premium beer. Expensive chocolates (traditionally one of those little luxuries we use to substitute for big ones in recessions) haven't fared so well this time round...but pineapple liquorice (eh?) is booming.

According to business information group IBISWorld's industry analyst, Richard Jeremiah (a voice crying in the wilderness, perhaps?), trends matter. This time round, he says, 'Buying habits are more mixed – people are cutting their spending on some items, but they won't compromise on others.'[12]

What's interesting, though, is the somewhat illogical way people go about prioritising their spending. You can understand how they'll cut

---

[12] www.theage.com.au/national/remedy-for-a-recession-20090307-8rz1.html

back on things they don't consider essential, such as plasma televisions and designer clothes...so how come we're suddenly going after pineapple liquorice?

So maybe if your plan is to open a fancy restaurant with fine wine and premium prices, then perhaps it's time for a rethink. But if you're planning to sell good, basic foodstuffs that customers can use to make their own delicious feasts right there at home, you needn't be too concerned and may even find you do better than you'd expected.

If you're planning to open a high class travel agency, reconsider. But if you're giving people a memorable experience they can have without travelling too far, then logic would suggest you're still going to be able to get going.

The point, then, is to **do your research**: make sure that you know how the GFC has hit your particular niche. Look at how this has been affected in previous downturns and how it's recovered afterwards. And then treat all your research with a little scepticism, because things change. (Magazines, for example, have traditionally thrived in recessions, the theory being that people can't afford big luxuries but can still dream with the help of a magazine for a couple of quid. This time round, however, they seem to have suffered – perhaps because there are other factors at play, like the Internet. We're just saying that what worked last time won't necessarily hold true this time round.)

And if, having done as much checking as you can, you decide to proceed, then check and double check that what you're doing is, as far as you can make it, recession-proof.

What does this mean? It means:

- being conservative with your **budgets** (can your business survive more costs and less income than you've budgeted for?);

- being stingy with your **cash flow** (if your customers don't pay on time, can you survive?);

- **spending nothing** you can avoid spending (do you need that big rental space, or can you manage on less?);

- **negotiating hard.** This isn't easy for everyone, but remember that when supply is up (lots of property on the market) and demand is down (fewer people desperate to buy), things are in your favour. Don't buy with the heart, but with the head;

- considering **different routes to market** that tend to do well in a recession, such as **party planning**, because it's easier in such tough times to recruit people who want to work from home and supplement the family income.

The great thing about all this is that, just like the businesses that have found the GFC has exposed their weaknesses, it makes you build a business that is strong enough to survive the worst of all worlds. If that's the case, imagine how fit your business will be when things ease up!

CHAPTER THIRTEEN

HELP! AND WHERE TO GET IT

"I would have liked to know more about: 1. Government programs for start-ups; 2. The networking groups that I now belong to; 3. Regulations and taxes!" Andy Roy, FInstIB NeXus Management Solutions

Here are nine words certain to chill any business person to the core: 'We're from the government…and we're here to help.' Yikes! Most of the time we think of the taxman and the government pretty much as we do the police: having anything to do with them is just about certain not to be good news. We'd be much happier going about our business and having as little to do with either set as we possibly can, thank you very much.

Well, think again, my friend. You, it may come as a surprise to discover, are the Engine Room of the Economy. You're What Makes This Country Great. You're the politician's best bloody mate and he bloody loves you, so he does. If he sees you in the street, he'll drop the baby he's currently harassing and throw his pudgy, work-shy, bribe-collecting arms around you and kiss your forehead with slobbery, wet lips (though not if you see him coming first, obviously).

However, before you get too big-headed about this, be aware that in fact this new-found regard is not so much for you and your funny, winsome ways, as for the fact that you are a Small Business, and governments just adore small businesses. They know that small businesses are what big businesses used to be and that besides, as we mentioned right back at the start of this book, they represent 99 per cent of all UK businesses.[13] Without you and your ilk, the Good Ship UK goes down, all hands on deck.

So there is a fair deal of help available for you, you'll be glad to know.

---

[13] www.hm-treasury.gov.uk/d/pbr08_economicengine_2390.pdf

Without question the place to start, and probably where you'll end up, too, is **www.businesslink.gov.uk**, the Government's all-purpose portal for transactions with business. Content-rich, accurate, up-to-date and inter-active – this is an extraordinarily good site that you need to put at the top of your 'To do' list. In particular there's an excellent Business Start-Up Organiser that really is the bee's knees.

For example, you can **check new business and brand names** against registers at Companies House (www.companieshouse.gov.uk) and the Intellectual Property Office (www.ipo.gov.uk). Put like that, it sounds simple and obvious – but believe us, if you ever had to do what was involved before, you'll be eternally grateful.

You can find out what regulations, licences and permits, trade bodies and standards apply to your particular type of business and do 101 other vital things that a start-up needs to do.

In fact, not only will you get great value out of this as you start your business, you'll also stick around to use it for things such as your quarterly VAT returns and all sorts of other compliance-type activities that profitable, thriving businesses get to do as punishment for being successful. (Not that we're cynical or anything.)

There's a nifty section on grants available to help out small-to-medium-sized businesses – like yours, perhaps. Well, indeed, what a good idea that would be. Grant eligibility is based on things like:

- **putting in a damn fine application that provides what they ask for;**

- **location – some underdeveloped areas have extra cash allocated;**

- **your size, industry sector and purpose (what are you going to do with the dosh, then?).**

At the time we looked, there were grants for rent relief in Sunderland and for historic building repairs in Cambridgeshire, and everything in between.

If grants are interesting to you, there are specialist grant advisers to help you put in applications – for the benefit of their health, of course (and, typically, a slice of the fee; but since it's success-based, you lose nothing by engaging them). Go to your favourite search engine and see what 'small business grant adviser' comes back with. Don't give anyone any money until you've thoroughly checked things out first, though! Actually there's enough info on www.businesslink.co.uk that you may not need much further help.

Anyway, stop reading this instant, go there now and see what we mean. Then come back and tell us we're wrong – we dare you.

Then, when you've sucked the juice out of Business Link, you can go to one of their regional advice sites, supported by a helpline (East of England, East Midlands, London, North West, North East, South East, South West, West Midlands and Yorkshire) – access yours via the main site. Wales has Flexible Support for Business (www.business-support-wales.gov.uk) and Northern Ireland, Invest Northern Ireland (www.investni.com). In Scotland, have a look at www.bgateway.com.

When you've done that, focus in on your own local council. They offer support and advice and lots of information on standards, applications and registrations, health and safety guidelines, local laws…spend some time having a crawl around.

Perhaps where these websites fall down is in lack of interactivity. Business Link has no blog (as there is at www.smallbusinesspro.co.uk, for example) and thus no sense of a small business community: it's very much one-way traffic, and working for yourself can leave you desperate for a bit of human interaction. Still, for all that, we can't recommend it highly enough. If it's bloggery you're after, head to www.sme-blog.com, http://community.zdnet.co.uk/small-business-blog (heavy IT bias) or the unhelpful mouthful that is www.allbusiness.com/business-planning-structures/starting-a-business/3882-1.html. Frankly, we feel the novelty wears off pretty quickly, though along the way you'll pick up some useful tips.

We also like Crimson Business's www.startups.co.uk, which has some pretty nifty content.

> **I am not made to work alone, I'd much rather work within a partnership/ business, provided I was able to enjoy a lot of autonomy and could keep learning new skills, improving the process, enjoying great teamwork. Running my own business can only provide that positive experience within a dynamic cohesive network of smart people with complementary skills experience and perspectives.** Francoise Garnier, Garnier Marketing Pty Ltd

What about in the real world? It's a lonely old life, so it is. Even if you have a business partner or two, a freelance HR help and a part-time bookkeeper, you might miss being part of a bigger organisation. To make some buddies and for peer support, try:

- **your peers** (meaning your competitors): stay friendly even if they make you a bit edgy. There will be people working in parallel businesses, not quite competitors, who you can have a brew with and pass the time of day without having to be too guarded;

- **industry groups, associations, community groups and cooperatives;**

- **local groups** such as traders' associations, small business cooperatives;

- having a look at your **local council website**; as well as support for businesses with information and support, as we mention above, they may well have a way of putting you in touch with similar souls in your neighbourhood.

There's also a tremendous book all about starting your own business that we recommend very highly, but you already know all about it. You're reading it.

CHAPTER FOURTEEN

PLANNING YOUR BUSINESS PLAN

> There are still 'feast and famine' aspects of consulting from an income planning point of view. Personal productivity is impacted by the needs of 'running a business', including filing, bookkeeping, tax returns, travel to client sites. All reduce the amount of 'productive' hours, and none are billable! Geoff Cutter, Melbourne Business Foundations

If you've never written a business plan in your life and the very thought fills you with worry, congratulations. By the end of this section you'll have your very own business plan – and a bloody good one, at that.

Business plans have had a bad rap, in our opinion, for three very different reasons. The **first reason** is that they're the staple of consultants, who can churn them out faster than you can write the cheque. All too often, what you're left with is a bog standard, highly detailed, absolutely useless document that you can never look at again without that sinking feeling as you think about the fun things you could have done with the money you spent on it. Why is it useless? Because it's not *yours*. It's still the consultant's – he or she has just got you to fill in the blanks.

We have a very different view. We think that you are different from him and different from her and you're *certainly* very different indeed from *them*. So why should your business plan look like his and hers and even theirs? Your business plan should look like *you*.

The **second reason** business plans have had a bad rap, we reckon, is that they are something most of us work on intensively for a bit then put to one side – or even worse, file – and never become part of the day-to-day life of our business.

Know this: if your business plan hasn't been touched in the past six months, it's out of date. And worse than being out of date, it's no longer part and parcel of your business's everyday life (if it ever was). So our approach, which we're just getting round to very shortly, takes care of that.

And the **third and final reason** for business plans stinking out the joint is that they're a good servant but a bad master. (GK Chesterton said that about alcohol: it's a good servant but a bad master. Neat, eh?) Meaning what, exactly? Meaning that they represent your current thinking about what's best for your business, rather than being a roadmap or a set of directions.

The objection, which we hear a fair bit, that 'there's no point in writing my business plan because things are changing so fast' is really not an objection at all so much as an excuse. Yes, things change – it would be pretty disappointing if in a year's time you didn't know more about your business than you do right now, wouldn't it? But no, that doesn't mean there's no point trying to summarise where you're at right now, where you think you want to get to next and how, right now, you reckon you're going to get there.

In fact, it's the very act of committing yourself, in writing, to your plan that helps you to develop it. You identify the weaknesses and the gaps; you also identify the strengths, the bits you're really convinced by. And you're saying you don't think identifying your gaps and your strengths is worthwhile? Pah! Tish and, if you don't mind us saying so, nonsense!

The fact of the matter is, you already have a business plan in your head.

Yes.
You.
Do.

If you have the vaguest notion of what your business is and the vaguest notion of where you want to go with it, then you already have a business plan. It's just...not a very good one. Yet. Soon, my good sweet-natured friend, soon.

Actually, tell you what, let's start right away. You need: a pulse, a pen and a piece of paper. And this book. Now, answer these questions, each in a single sentence and in no more than 30 seconds. (That's right, we really do want you to rush into this and we really don't want you to think it through. Have a crack: you'll be amazed.)

It comes in four parts: about the product; about making the product; about marketing the product, and about funding your business.

PART A: ABOUT THE PRODUCT

1. What is the potential for this business?
Simple one, straight off the bat. Where do you think this business is headed? Is it going to be a shop, for example, a chain of shops, a franchise or a Tesco killer?

_____

_____

2. Why would someone buy your thing rather than someone else's?
If you've got something about your product or service that is attractive, write it down. If you don't, you have a problem.

_____

_____

3. How and where would someone buy it?
Are they buying it from a shop, online, in person or what?

_____

_____

4. When is it going to be available?
Tough one – but take a guess. Is it going to take you a year to get on sale? Probably not. Will it be on sale this afternoon? Probably not. So you've narrowed it down; now narrow it down further – three months, six months, nine months?

_____

_____

PART B: ABOUT MAKING THE PRODUCT

1. Is this a product that (a) will be massively cheaper to make once you're making heaps; or (b) will the 100th cost the same as the first?

Example of the former: *a cardboard box, a bottle, a copy of a book*

Example of the latter: *a personal training session or a massage*

_____

_____

2. Are you (a) able to get someone else to take the risk of making these things; or are you (b) going to have to take on the risk (and reap the reward) of making them yourself?

Example of the former: *a cardboard box, a bottle, a copy of a book*

Example of the latter: *a book written by you (yes, you could use a ghost-writer – but even there it's your name and your reputation on the cover)*

_____

_____

3. How easy will it be for others to copy what you're doing? Will it be (a) very difficult indeed; or will it be (b) very simple?

Example of the former: *anything that can be protected, such as intellectual property (copyright, patent etc); that has something you can keep secret (such as the Coca Cola recipe) or that is intimately bound up with your own identity or personality (such as being Gordon Ramsay)*

Example of the latter: *any 'widget' or manufactured item that can (i.e. will) be ripped off in a factory on the other side of the world*

_____

_____

4. Is this thing as yet unmade? Are you going to have to spend (a) a ton of time and money to turn an idea/prototype into a shelf-ready product? Or are you (b) dealing with something already there, or as near as dammit?

Example of the former: *a brainwave of your own devising, that is just so obviously going to succeed you can't understand how everyone else has missed it*

Example of the latter: *something that was just so obviously going to succeed that someone else didn't miss it, so they have already built it; and now you get to sell it*

_____

_____

PART C: ABOUT MARKETING THE PRODUCT AND SELLING IT

1. Do you know, or think you know, what it's going to take to promote this product?

If this question makes you squirm a little, don't be discouraged. If you have strong ideas and you just don't know how well they're going to work, and that's why you're squirming, then at least you've given it some thought. If, however, you're squirming a great deal because you haven't given this any thought up until this point, or you're not squirming at all because you don't see why this matters, then you need to pause and take stock. It's not as if you can't make a product successful if you don't know how to promote it – it's just that you're certainly taking the hard route, and one that very few otherwise excellent products survive.

_____

_____

2. When you are bringing your product to the attention of your potential customers, where are you going to put your effort and money into advertising and promoting it?

Online? Yellow Pages? Leaflets delivered door to door? Signage for passers by? Networking? Party planning (i.e. you get people to sell your stuff for commission to others at social events)? See Chapter 11 for ideas.

_____

_____

3. When you have succeeded in finding a customer, do you know how they will perceive your product?

This is trickier than it sounds. Most of the time we buy at an emotional level, based on many subconscious drives and beliefs, so asking people how they buy (and therefore appealing to their conscious, cognitive minds) isn't necessarily the best way to find out. Famous example: ask people why they buy tyres and they'll tell you it's safety, when in fact they buy mostly on price. A more effective way of learning how customers really perceive your product is to conduct a pilot test and talk to them after they've already bought (an early version) of it.

_____

_____

4. Do you have a superb marketing strategy?

Are you going to be famous for your prices (cheap or expensive), your service or for something else? Do you know who your customers are and how you're going to reach them? Are you going to build a world-class website, a cheap one or none at all? (See Chapter 11 for more on all this stuff.)

_____

_____

PART D: ABOUT FUNDING YOUR BUSINESS

1. Have you done a cash-flow projection?

There's one powerful and irreplaceable reality check: how long will your cash last? If you're developing a product, have you enough money to keep you going while you do so, so that you're not relying on revenue from sales to come at the earliest possible point? Here's a tip: sales won't come at the earliest possible point. Murphy and Sod loved each other very, very much in a special way and together they made a little Law especially for you. No, we can't tell you what will prevent your sales coming at the earliest possible point – we can just tell you that they won't.

_____

_____

2. When things develop a wobble (and they will), have you a Plan B to enable you to get funds that you currently don't anticipate requiring?

Are we being unduly pessimistic? We are very optimistic that we are, and that your Plan B can get you through safely. Think of it as being like insurance – something you hope never to use – with this difference: having a Plan B won't cost you anything. NOT having a Plan B, now THAT can be seriously, indeed ruinously, expensive.

3. Have you two (or more) projects that you're developing?

You have an enterprising, entrepreneurial mind – that you're reading this book at all shows that. But the downside is that sometimes you have so many great ideas that you can't resist the temptation to have more than one on the go.

Play a game. The rule is simple: pretend you had to choose just one of these projects. Which would it be? Now, stop playing the game and get real: DROP everything else, right now. Concentrate all your mighty powers and effort and concentration and will on your one best project.

(There's a theme here. Many businesses make two mistakes: heading in more than one direction and not having a fallback plan. You can out-think and out-perform them just by reversing those polarities: go hard in a single direction – and have a Plan B.)

4. Do you have the support and help of those around you?

Think about the concept of the 'Hidden Decision Maker' (HDM), which may be your husband/wife or someone else. You're going to need them onside, and if they're not with you already, you need to work on this. One of the very best things you can do is to create a detailed written plan, show it to your HDM, ask for advice – and take it. Our experience has been that two heads really are better than one – and of course if you're sharing responsibility, you're far more likely to have their support.

A WORD ON BUSINESS STRUCTURE

We assume you're planning to be self-employed (a reasonable assumption, given the nature of this book). Your simplest option is to be a **sole trader**; if you're working together with another person you may wish to form a **partnership**. The next step up is to create a **limited liability partnership** (LLP), which gives you some protection if things don't work out, because it means that your liability is limited to the money you've invested in the business plus any personal guarantees you give to raise finances. However, you may wish to establish a **private limited liability company**, which means that the company's finances are separate from yours as a shareholder.

So which do you choose and what are the consequences? That's a big question and one we're not qualified to answer, even if we did have room. Best place to start, as so often with these things, is at www.businesslink.gov. uk and click on 'Starting up' on the lefthand menu. Eventually you'll need financial and legal advice and you really mustn't plough on without it; the cost of getting advice is massively outstripped by the cost of getting it wrong.

Now, we have to admit that what you've created here isn't what consultants usually have in mind when they're talking about a business plan and it *certainly* isn't what your bank manager has in mind when she talks about a business plan. But the great news is, you've already identified all the key challenges that you face and, in many cases, your current best answer as to how you're going to address them.

The even better news is, you don't need to spend very much time at all now turning that information into a tight, clear, highly effective business plan that:

- gives your business **more focus and energy** than ever before;

- comes in mighty handy for **measuring progress**;

- is exactly what your **bank manager** wants to see from you.

It's not there yet and you're not quite ready to go running off to your bank manager: you need flesh on those bones first. There's a format to a business plan for a bank manager and the above isn't it. But fret not, because long before you need to go to her with one, you'll have a very clear idea indeed of what she needs. Trust us.

Talking to your bank manager and other not very sympathetic people

When it does become time to approach your bank manager, there are a few things you need to bear in mind. First and foremost, despite everything that's happened in the world in the past couple of years, the truth is that your bank manager wants to do business with you. She really does. Her bank doesn't make its vast billions from *not* doing business, after all.

Even more than wanting to do business with you, however, she really, really, *really* doesn't want to lend money to a business venture that doesn't even know how to get her to lend money to it. If she does so, and it's obvious from the paperwork that she should have seen you coming, then it's second customer service from the far end at the Smethwick branch for her, and no way back

It's a game, if you like: you show us you know how to ask for money properly and we'll lend it to you. Alternatively, you have a great business idea but absolutely bugger all idea how to win over your bank manager, so we'll keep the drawer with the chequebook in locked, OK?

And while there are all the usual jokes about banks only lending money to people (and businesses) who don't need it, that's actually not true. It would be more accurate to say that banks only lend money to people (and businesses) who can make a convincing case that they'll be able to pay it back. Which is fair enough, when you think about it. Of course, that's not the same as saying you have to *prove* you can pay it back – you can't predict the future and neither can anyone else – just that you have to do the best you can.

So what makes a convincing case, then? Well, here are five issues your bank manager will have in her mind when you come round with the hat:

1. What's your track record like?

Although financial institutions are fond of reminding us that the past is no predictor of the future and shares may go down as well as up (remember when shares used to go up?), it makes sense for your bank manager to see how good you've been at paying your debts. Ask yourself:

- **Do I have a good credit history?**
- **Have I filed all my income tax returns?**
- **Have I paid my income tax?**

2. Can you repay us?

She wants you to pay back the money you borrow, plus interest. Ask yourself:

- **Is the business profitable?**
- **Is it growing?**
- **Can I show how the business will pay this money back?**

3. Are you committed, as opposed to just being involved? Do you have 'skin in the game'?

You can hardly sit there telling your bank manager what a fabulous opportunity this is if you don't have enough belief in it to put your own money where your mouth is. Well, OK, you can: see how far it gets you. Ask yourself:

- Egg or bacon? (Old joke: with an egg, the chicken is involved; when it comes to bacon, the pig is committed.)
- Am I willing to personally guarantee the loan?

4. Do you have collateral?

Business assets or personal assets, she'll take either. But she needs to know what to come and take away in a van if you can't meet your commitments.

5. Are you experienced?

This hardly seems fair. But if you had a quid to lend, either to a complete novice or someone who'd been round the block a couple of times, where would you put it? However, all is not lost, because at least if you have qualified advisers (such as a financial adviser or an accountant) or a qualified manager involved in the business, then you don't have to do it all by yourself.

Have good answers for that little lot, and you're well on the way.

Before you think about this stuff, by the way, here's a key question – do you actually *need* to borrow money? If you're trotting off to talk to your bank manager because you can't possibly start a business without a personal assistant, a BMW and a very swanky office and you need to borrow the cash to get all that, you're probably reading the wrong book. As you'll have gathered, we much prefer to keep overheads low. And if you think this is a ridiculous thing for us to say and that no one would be that daft, then, well, you clearly haven't met some of the failed business owners we've met.

If you're not too sure…read on.

Coming up next – business plan template. That's where you make all this stuff suitable for viewing by others.

CHAPTER FIFTEEN

BUSINESS PLAN TEMPLATE

> **I guess I'm very committed to our 'organic growth' model. I know other people who've started with plans and paperwork and position descriptions and investors and have forgotten what it's actually all about.**
> Rose Michael, Arcade Publications

Now comes the time to transfer all that good stuff you've already created into a standard business plan format. There's a lot of them around, as 30 seconds with Google will show you. We'll take you through one in a moment, but if you don't like ours there'll be another one along shortly if you just go paddling around the interwebs for a few minutes.

Hot tip: do NOT go spending money on buying a business plan template. You really, honestly and truly don't need to go splashing your hard-earned cash on this stuff, and in our experience nothing you pay for will give you anything you can't get here or from countless other free plans.

In our view – and we're happy to argue the toss with you on this – a business plan template is such a simple, straightforward, common-sense document that anyone who charges for one actually needs to find a better business model for themselves, since it shows remarkable short-termism to ask people to pay for what is effectively public domain. Heaven knows, there's enough advice and assistance required by anyone running a business that there should be plenty of opportunities to add value. Of course if you claim to have something special and new about your business plan template then please, go right ahead. It's right up there with the better mousetrap…

BUSINESS PLAN
by
[Name, address, contact details]
[Date]

PART 1: THE BUSINESS
Our name
The proposed name for the business is *[name]*

_____

Our big idea
The business idea is *[describe]*

_____

_____

_____

Where
The business will be based at *[my home/workshop premises/shop premises/ office premises/other]*

_____

_____

_____

Our key success factors
[Describe the background to the business idea and the reasons why it will succeed. State whether similar businesses already exist in your area along with your advantage over them, or whether this is an original product/service which no other businesses in your local area already offer.]

_____

_____

_____

_____

_____

Strengths and weaknesses

[List here your strengths and weaknesses – for example, location, resources, reputation, services, people etc. Remember though that a strength is only a strength if you are better at it than your competitors: otherwise it's just not a weakness.]

Strengths	Weaknesses
1	1
2	2
3	3
4	4

Our people: customers

[Describe in fine detail your typical customer – or examples of your typical customers. Give them a name, an address, an age, an occupation: make them come alive. Say why this invented person – your customer – will be attracted to your business rather than others.]

_____

_____

_____

_____

Our people: business partners

[Describe business partners, including skills, qualifications and experience, and the roles each of you perform.]

_____

_____

_____

_____

Our skills and abilities

[List the skills, qualifications and abilities you have which contribute to your business's success. Include previous jobs or businesses. Sell yourself hard!]

_____

_____

_____

_____

_____

_____

Our people: staff and employees

[Give numbers and types of key staff and employees you plan to recruit. Be sure to include the principal roles and positions which need to be filled.]

_____

_____

_____

_____

_____

_____

PART 2: MARKETING

What we are going to be famous for

[State what you want people to recommend you to their friends for. If you're a butcher, for example, will your selling point be range? Quality? Friendly service? Cheap prices? If you think you'll be able to achieve expensive things like quality and service and undercut the market on price, then this is a great place to explain how you're going to pull that off. Not that we're sceptical or anything. It's just that...well, you know, it's a pretty rare combination.]

_____

_____

_____

_____

_____

_____

How we are going to get famous

[List all the ways we're going to promote our business and what each will cost. This figure will total the figure that is going into the first line of your expenditure in Part 3b, 'Costs: advertising and promotion'. This is the most important part of the whole plan – there's no point in having a great business idea if you can't get the word around.]

_____

_____

_____

_____

_____

PART 3a: FUNDING AND INCOME

Capital available from savings and investments

The savings and investments which I/we are putting into the business are *[state amount]*

_____

_____

_____

I/we also plan to raise additional capital of *[amount]* from *[say where you will raise this from]*

_____

_____

_____

Income from sales

I/we estimate that income from sales will be:

First six months: *[amount]*
Second six months: *[amount]*
[say how you're going to get these sales]

_____

_____

Grants and training support available
[State any you know about for which you may be eligible]

_____

_____

_____

Security
I/we have available these assets as potential security against loans:

Market value of home: *[amount]*
Less outstanding mortgage: *[amount]*
Less other loans secured on home: *[amount]*
Estimated equity in home: *[amount]*

Security available from other sources: *[amount]*

Start-up loan
[If you believe you need it, state amount]

PART 3b: COSTS
Pay
I/we plan to pay ourselves:

First six months: *[amount]*
Second six months: *[amount]*

Costs

I/we expect to incur expenditure as follows:

	Before launch	First six months	Second six months
Advertising and promotion	[amount]	[amount]	[amount]
Computers			
Despatch costs			
Equipment			
Fixtures and fittings			
Gas/electricity			
Insurance			
Machinery			
Print, stationery			
Professional fees			
Rates			
Rent			
Raw materials			
Telephone			
Wages [exclude yours]			
Vehicles			
Fuel costs, road tax			
Other [list]			
Total	[amount]	[amount]	[amount]

Capital costs

I/we need to finance the following items of capital equipment during the first year of the business:

Cars [list quantity]:	*[amount]*
Commercial vehicles:	*[amount]*
Computer equipment:	*[amount]*
Equipment:	*[amount]*
Machinery:	*[amount]*
Office equipment:	*[amount]*
Office furnishings:	*[amount]*
Others [list others]:	*[amount]*
Total:	***[amount]***

Finance payments

I/we estimate the total cost of finance payments will be:

First six months: *[amount]*
Second six months: *[amount]*

Costs for materials

I/we need to buy the following types and quantities of materials:

_____

_____

_____

I/we estimate that these materials will cost approximately *[x]* per cent of the price at which we expect to be able to sell the finished products.

_____

[Note: this is called your 'gross margin'. Get it right and get used to it: you're going to be spending a lot of time with this number!]

PART 3c: CASH-FLOW PROJECTION

We reckon that a robust cash-flow projection spreadsheet is likely to be one of your most valuable business tools. 'Cash-flow projection', by the way, merely means predicting how your finances are going to look over time. Typically a business will go heavily into the red early on, when your start-up costs are at their heaviest and before you've got substantial revenues coming in from sales. If you're not ready for this, you'll run out of cash before you give the business a chance to get going. You should talk to your accountant and other qualified financial advisers about this. It may cost you to find out how your cash flow is going to hold up – but not nearly as much as it costs to find out the hard way!

We thought about creating you a cash-flow projection template, except actually you don't want one in this book, you want one on your computer. So here you go. There are plenty of cash-flow projection templates on the Web. Here are two free options (addresses were correct at the time of writing):

Microsoft Office Template
office.microsoft.com/en-au/templates/TC011132361033.aspx
Good, straightforward template that should get you going

Business Link UK Template
www.businesslink.gov.uk/Finance_files/Cash_Flow_Projection_Worksheet_v2.xls
Wow. Just…wow. This is seriously good stuff. First class guidelines and explanations for what's going on. You can't do much better than this, without having someone write you a tailored version for your particular business.

Don't panic if this bit looks a bit serious; by following the guidelines and using your superb brains, even if you stuff some of it up, you'll be doing better than 97 per cent of the start-ups out there.

Away you go then. Best of British.

CHAPTER SIXTEEN

SOME WAYS TO IMPROVE YOUR ODDS

Or, The ten really crap habits of failed entrepreneurs

It takes guts, it takes longer than you think, the market will always surprise you, but it is worth it over and over! Johan Venter, JPV Business Solutions

This chapter presents the hard-won wisdom of those who've gone before. Hard-won, we say, because in many cases the mistakes they made have cost them businesses, not to mention houses and spouses. Look at it this way: follow the wisdom captured here, avoid their mistakes – and if you're going to fail, you're going to have find brand new ways to do so. Still quite possible, of course: but harder.

Here are ten mistakes to avoid:

Mistake Number One: Putting all your eggs in one basket

Mistake Number Two: Hedging your bets

Hang on a minute. Stop right there. What has probably struck you about the first two Mistakes to Avoid, if you're paying any kind of attention at all, is that they're completely self-contradictory. If risking everything is a mistake and *not* risking everything is a mistake, how the Dickens are you supposed to avoid falling into one of these two mutually contradictory holes?

Ah well, you see, it's all to do with context. If you have options that enable you to move into your chosen business and limit the risk, then you should definitely keep your options open (hedge your bets). On the other hand, if by doing so you're not giving your business the chance to succeed, and you're also not really committing to it, then perhaps you need to go all out to make it work (and thus put all your eggs in one basket). It's really just a case of being very honest with yourself and following Kenny Roger's advice in 'The Gambler': *You got to know when to hold 'em, know when to fold 'em/Know when to walk away and know when to run*. If keeping our options open actually means not allowing ourselves to succeed, then it's time to commit; on the other hand, if we are rashly risking everything on a very risky venture, then it's time to recognise the danger.

Let's illustrate with a couple of examples.

"**Huge stress for the first 18 months. Cash-flow problems, early on anyway. Got bad advice about business structure and had to re-do it after two years!** Robert Hamilton-Jones, Business Advantage International

"**Timing is a huge problem for us because we're so small and a start-up we can turn on a dime – so we keep forgetting how slow everyone else is!** Rose Michael, Arcade Publications

The point is, you can't get half-pregnant. Either you're in this, boots and all, for better or for worse, for richer or for poorer – or you're mucking about. As seven-times world snooker champion Stephen Hendry put it (and he should know), 'if you are not committed mentally, you might as well give up'.

And we don't, on the whole and taking all things into consideration, recommend mucking about. We love this story about the legendary Liverpool football manager Bill Shankly, which says so much about motivation, of oneself and of others:

> If I became a bin-man tomorrow, I'd be the greatest bin-man who ever lived. I'd have Liverpool the cleanest city on Earth. I'd have everyone working with me, succeeding and sharing out the success. I'd make sure they were paid a decent wage with the best bonuses and that we all worked hard to achieve our goals.
>
> Some people might say, 'ah but they're only bin-men, why do we need to reward them so well for a job anyone can do', but I'd ask them why

they believe they are more important than a bin-man.

I'd ask them how proud they'd feel if this dirty city became the cleanest in the world? And who would have made them proud? The bin-men.[14]

However, if you *are* committed, then you need to give yourself every chance to succeed. It's all very well to feel that nothing motivates you to drag in the cash like an overdue mortgage payment, and if you're someone who responds well to a deadline then the threat of losing the house is a pretty good one. But any business needs cash, and the cash takes time to arrive, time that you may very well not have.

Yes, these first two Mistakes are mutually contradictory, and it really is just a case of recognising the dangers in both, and making sure you steer between them.

Mistake Number Three: Letting your emotion cloud your judgement

A really good example of this is a retail business. You can have the best stuff in your shop and the best prices – but if no one can park within half a mile of your shop, you've had it. So when you look at a retail site, you need to, as the poet WB Yeats put it, 'cast a cold eye', divorced from emotion and even need. If you HAVE to find a site, you're far more likely to see the positives in what you're looking at – and that's fine, so long as you don't blind yourself to the potential downsides.

Mistake Number Four: Not setting your goals

If you don't know where you're going, you're in danger of setting off down any old road, which may – or more likely, may not – get you there. (Plus you won't know when you've arrived.) Without wishing to generalise, the British are terrible at this and Americans are great at it. (OK perhaps there's an element of generalisation there. Just a tad.) We're not entirely sure why this is, but perhaps it's something to do with the essentially optimistic nature of Americans – the American Dream, no less. It is, after all, (relatively speaking) a recently colonised country, one which has had the benefit of massive

---

[14] www.mirror.co.uk/sport/columnists/reade

influxes of millions of immigrants throughout the nineteenth and twentieth centuries. This created so many inspiring stories of men and women who arrived with nothing and made their fortune. The British, by contrast, have been around much longer – centuries, and even millennia. Perhaps there's something in the British national character that is wary of too much gungho optimism, all that razzmatazz and 'Just do it' spirit?

And yet, if you *don't* set out with clear goals in mind, the chances of you achieving them are greatly reduced – and this chapter is, after all, supposed to be about increasing your odds. There is much evidence, which we're far too busy to Google for you, to show that entrepreneurs and business people who set goals are generally much more likely to be successful, rich and married to really hot partners.

Mistake Number Five: Not setting the right goals
So if it makes sense to provide some formal motivation, then it makes even more sense to provide the *right* formal motivation. Set your sights too low and you'll limit what you can achieve. As the aforementioned Bill Shankly used to put it, 'Aim for the sky and you may just hit the ceiling. Aim for the ceiling and you'll end up on your back.' So it is important to set yourself an ambitious target – and even if you don't quite achieve it, you'll still have gone a lot further than if you aimed too low.

However, if setting a goal is all there were to it, we'd all set ourselves the goal of, say, making a billion by bedtime. Ain't gonna happen. Aim for achievable or you're destined for disappointment.

So if goals mustn't be too low and mustn't be too high and must, indeed, be juuuust right (this is beginning to sound like the three bears' porridge), then how the hell are you supposed to know they are appropriate or not?

The best way we know is to make them SMART, which stands for:

- **Specific**
- **Measurable**
- **Ambitious**
- **Realistic**
- **Timely**

(There are several variations on what SMART stands for. We like 'ambitious' rather than the more common 'attainable', since we think that's pretty well covered in 'realistic'. Don't write to us to discuss this, because we don't care. Use what works for you.) Test your goals against these criteria. Let's go through them one by one.

It's been found that setting yourself a specific target works much better than something vague and woolly. 'I sincerely want to be rich' isn't specific, since what you or I would regard as rich, Richard Branson or Bill Gates might regard as loose change. 'I want to make a million', however, is specific and measurable. (Actually, even there it's important to state what you mean, in very specific terms. It isn't hard for a business to *turn over* a million and yet not be profitable. So if by 'make' you mean net, that's fine. Just be clear to yourself what you're aiming for, is all.)

'I want to make a million' isn't, however, timely. When by? In 40 years, you may very well make your first million – but it won't be enough to retire on. 'I want to make my first million in six months time' is, probably, unrealistic. 'I want to make my first million in four years time' is more like it. It's certainly specific, it's measurable, it's (reasonably) ambitious, it's realistic and it's timely (meaning that there's a built-in deadline).

The reason why all this is so important is that you are driven by your internal and external motivations, and unless you are crystal clear about what they are, you won't tap into the full power of your resources.

Mistake Number Six: Not writing down your goals

Sheesh, you may well be saying to yourself at this point, they're really banging on and on a bit about the old goals aren't they? OK, we get it already.

But there's not a whole lot of point in setting goals, even if they're the right ones, if you don't write them down. Along with a capacity to laugh, use language and oppose thumbs, it appears that one of the characteristics that marks out Homo sapiens from the rest of the animal kingdom is the ability to self-deceive. If we're honest we've all been guilty at one time or another of rewriting history, fudging the facts, shuffling the deck and generally retro-spectively amending things in our own favour. And that's fine – in fact, it's far better than the alternative, which is to drive yourself mad with regret.

Even better than either of these options, however, is to commit yourself to your vision. In writing. Go away by yourself. Write it down. Date it. (We password the document, so we know we're the only beings on earth who get to see these goals.) And revisit it regularly – once a quarter, perhaps.

Mistake Number Seven: Not turning your goals into an action plan

So you have your goals (something to aim for) and they're the right ones (they're specific, measurable, ambitious, realistic and timely) and they're written down right in front of you. Go for these and you'll find they pull you forward – it's almost as if your subconscious is dragging you towards what it knows you want. (Funny that, because that's exactly what's happening.) Is that enough? No.

Now you need to build a line to travel along between two points – those points being this moment and your end point. Let's assume your end point is two and a half years away. Thirty months. One hundred and thirty weeks. Nine hundred and ten days. Take away weekends, holidays, time off of various kinds and you're talking not much more than, say, seven hundred days. A week, then, makes up a whole percentage point of the time available to you. So what you need to do now is to build a plan, so that when you're half way there in time, you're also at the right point along in your execution of your plan. Note that being half way through in terms of time doesn't necessarily mean being half way there in terms of your goal – it may do, or it may not. What is important is that you know what your path is and what the milestones are along the way.

It sounds insultingly easy, doesn't it? Well, it may be easy but that doesn't mean that many people follow this recipe. Actually we believe this is the sort of thing they should teach in schools and certainly at university – but that's another story (and we're working on it).

By the way, we've heard too many people dismiss this planning as unworkable, because 'things change'. Yes, indeed they do. And in one sense these people are quite right: you won't follow the path you've set, at the speed you've set, to the end point you've set. For one thing, do you really and honestly believe you won't have changed over the course of the next two and half years? If that is the case, then frankly we'd have to say you've wasted a fair chunk of your life. OF COURSE you'll change, perhaps more in this period than you have over the past decade or more. And as you change, so too do the things you regard as important – and the things you don't. So, for example, you may find that actually spending time with your young family becomes more (or less) important to you over this period – and that, naturally, will tend to change your plans. So what? Does that mean you shouldn't make plans? Does it mean that, because your views change, the ones you held originally were wrong or bad? Of course not. Indeed, quite the opposite: it's a sign of growth. Therefore it makes no logical sense to say that, because you change and so too do your plans, then you shouldn't make any. Which, in the way of these things, brings us right on to...

Mistake Number Eight: Making your servant your master

GK Chesterton (him again) described alcohol as a good servant but a bad master, and your plans are like that. Their purpose is to guide you, to give you something to go towards, to help you clarify why you're doing all this and to enable you to find your path. They are emphatically not there to limit you, and you mustn't let them.

Actually in one sense they *are* there to limit you. They give you focus and should make you think twice, and then twice again, about taking on another big project at the same time. You only have room for one and this one is it. The other thing you can do later, when you've got this one up and running. But this single sense apart, your plans are there to give you clarity and focus – and at any time you like you can change that focus and shift it elsewhere, and you can be just as clear about something else instead...if you so choose. And that's the point. If you want to, you can rip up your plan and write another one or, more likely, you can amend your current one in the light of new information. Let's take an absurd example. Suppose that the whole world economy goes down the pan and all the certainties you've been working with for the past 20 years fall to bits. Never going to happen, of course – don't be silly! – but just imagine that it did. Well, your plan would need to change too, wouldn't it?

Mistake Number Nine: Forgetting your plan

There's a peculiar aspect to this planning that needs to be pointed out. It's very much like the way writing something down to remember it helps you remember it – so next time you don't write it down and then you forget. Create your plan and write it down, and it rapidly becomes so familiar to you and so much part of your thinking that you then forget to go back to it, to consult it, to revisit it and renew it. That's the danger time. Because then you start to edit it in your own mind, without noticing that's what you're doing. You start leaving off the hard bits and going soft on your milestones. You let yourself off the hook, in other words – and that's something that your plan will never do for you. It sits there, remembering all, forgiving and forgetting nothing. Actually it can be very annoying indeed – it's almost as if your plan is silently rebuking you or holding you accountable. That indeed *is* what it's doing, because it's a reminder to you of your best you, the highest-achieving you, the hardest-working you: the you you need to be, as much of the time as humanly possible, if you are to make this thing succeed.

Mistake Number Ten: You don't read this book

OK, that's one mistake you're not going to make. Hurrah for you! Now what about the other nine?

CHAPTER SEVENTEEN

TEN COMMON PITFALLS: WHICH ONE WILL YOU FALL INTO?

We've already talked at some length about the mistakes others who've gone before you have made, and how to avoid them. This chapter sniffs out the clues that reveal which kind of failure you're most prone to. Don't be alarmed, by the way, by all this talk of 'mistakes' and 'failure'. To our way of thinking, the very best way to guarantee your success is to be brutally honest about those things about yourself of which you need to be most aware. There's absolutely nothing wrong with having weak spots. We all do. Think about Richard Branson, Alan Sugar, Anita Roddick, Bill Gates or Rupert Murdoch for a second and you'll quickly see the kind of characteristics they possess that have put them under pressure on more than one occasion.

So this chapter is the 'know thyself' one. It may be that your particular flaw is to be terrible at managing people or a difficulty in controlling your emotions or a tendency to worry yourself sick. Whatever it is, the more you know about yourself, the better you can adapt and manage your way around your own particular weaknesses.

Your authors here, Susannah and Steve, make a nice illustration of this point, because our faults (as well as our virtues) are complementary. Steve is one of nature's improvisers, working best up against a tight deadline when the chips are down. Big picture sort of a chap. Downside: he's hopeless at paperwork and detail (pitfall number two below). Susannah's quite the opposite, exceptionally good at the detail and making sure that things get done. Downside: she's a perfectionist, which means that she tends to torture herself unnecessarily rather than making do (pitfall number eight below). We're acutely aware of our faults and failings and in part that's why we work so well together, because we can compensate for each other.

Before we start, a word of warning: if you honestly and truly don't recognise yourself, even just a bit, in any of these little portraits, then one of three things is going on. Either we've missed out your particular weakness (which is fine, in the sense that if you're aware of it that's all that matters) or alternatively you're absolutely perfect (in which case what on earth are you doing reading a book that's intended to help you make yourself better?) or, last and most likely, you're not nearly as self-aware as you imagine yourself to be. And that's where the need for the warning comes in, because if that is true, you're going to struggle big time. It's one thing to have faults, it's another entirely not even to be aware that you have them. That way danger lies.

Anyway, we reckon it's fairly unlikely you won't see yourself here. After all, you have the wisdom as well as the lack of arrogance to have picked up this book and that shows that you don't think you know it all. That's a great place to start!

So let's go meet some folk.

Common Pitfall Number One: Mr Terrible Manager

He is: almost certainly someone you've worked for. You know the type, and he or she is almost certainly the reason why you're now working for yourself. Swift to criticise, stingy with praise. Suspicious. Untrustworthy. Impossible to please. Easy to get on the wrong side of. Prone to moodiness. Inconsistent. Grumpy. Plays favourites. Sets a terrible example. Never heard a good idea unless it was (suddenly, mysteriously, after the event) his own. Bad-mannered. Pedantic. Claims to do business on a handshake – when (and only when) it suits him. Cynical. Bully.

This is troubling, for one simple reason: he'd never recognise himself from this picture. He reckons he's the epitome of reasonableness (or would, if he could say it). He may admit to playing hard, but insists he plays fair. And if he doesn't recognise himself, then *how do you know you're not like that yourself?*

Lesson: Work at your interpersonal skills. Be swift to give praise and slow to take credit. Keep cheerful. Be consistent and consistently nice. Think about what you say before you say it. Let your word be your bond and never go back on a handshake.

Common Pitfall Number Two: Ms Terrible Paperwork

She is: an absolute shambles. Never keeps notes or records. Has a diary, but never opens it. Actually has three diaries and they all say different things. Doesn't know her own phone number, let alone anyone else's. Has far more contact with the tax office than is healthy, because she's miles behind on everything.

   Lesson: If this sounds like you, don't avoid the obvious. Don't think you can change, because you can't. You can get just about acceptably good at this stuff – for a while – and then you'll revert to type. Instead, get yourself the right kind of support: a bookkeeper and an accountant, for starters. They'll cost you a fair bit, but not nearly as much as not having them will cost you. And while you'll never be a high scorer at paperwork, even you really can manage a decent diary. Be religious about keeping it up – and consult it every evening prior to the following day.

Common Pitfall Number Three: Mr Addictive Risk-Taker

He is: a gambler by nature. Instead of betting on the nags or the black, however, he's sublimated his risk-taking into his business. He is happiest going all out, staking everything on a gamble that, if it pays off, pays off big – the operative word being that *if*, of course.

   Lesson: No good will come of it. The Global Financial Crisis has uncovered many, many financiers and entrepreneurs who ignored all advice and put everything with something that promptly sank without trace. Now they have had to sell up and are living in a one-room bedsit with their mum. Either that or they blew their brains out (and, faced with the alternative, we can't say we blame them). The thing is, if you play so you have to be lucky all the time, eventually you won't be – and then it's all gone. It's not worth the risk and you need to be sure that you're taking decisions with a clear head and a cold eye. Listen to your accountant, who'll tell you to spread your risk and not put all your eggs in one basket (she may even use this very phrase).

Common Pitfall Number Four: Ms Self-Defeater

She is: bound to fail, obviously. How can she not? This isn't just Ms Glass Half-Full, this is Ms Yes and It's Probably Got Typhoid Germs in It, Too. Talk about negative! Talk about always expecting the worst! And of course, the more she expects things to go wrong, the more she's not disappointed. At one level she's probably trying to protect herself from disappointment, not letting herself jinx the future by hoping too much and preparing herself for the worst. Yet being in the company such a downbeat, deadbeat, downright depressing person is murder for everyone around.

Lesson: Oh cheer *up* for God's sake. Yes, things may go wrong. But since the future is not yet written, except in our own minds, why on earth would we choose to inhabit and populate such a miserably downbeat one? What's wrong with hoping for the best and believing that things not only can but will turn out well? In this life you don't necessarily get what you deserve – but you certainly find what you're looking for.

Common Pitfall Number Five: Mr Stress Head

He is: a close relation of Ms Self-Defeater above. Mr Stress Head is carrying the weight of the world on his shoulders. His motto? Anything that can go wrong will. Sod's Law, Murphy's Law...it's all bound to go to hell in a handcart sooner or later, and only Mr Stress Head can postpone the inevitable. He's the one tearing around trying to do everything, unable to depend on anyone, unable to trust anyone. And when things go wrong, as inevitably they will if it's all in the hands of one man, well, then that just goes to show how everyone else is letting him down by 'making' him take it all on himself.

Lesson: You can't do everything yourself and if you try, you'll burst. Deep down there may be a certain insecurity here, as if by having good people around, you end up looking less good yourself. Actually the opposite is true: if you have fantastic folk around you, they'll make you look great. They'll be a credit to you and they will make life bearable and probably make you a stack of money. Of course, if it was just as easy as all that, then Mr Stress Head would instantly cease to exist. Unfortunately it isn't that easy. Still and all, there's a little of Mr Stress Head about each of us, so if we can reduce our inclination to take on too much and not trust people, we should do so.

Common Pitfall Number Six: Ms Gadfly

She is: the world's best 100m sprinter – in marathons. At home she has a ton of sporting equipment: skis, from the one season she skiied; diving equipment, from the one time she got into scuba; guns, from when she took up shooting...all now gathering dust. At work she's exactly the same. She's a Monday Morning Genius, when a 'brilliant, absolutely brilliant' idea sparks off a rush of enthusiasm that rarely if ever sees out the week. There's a stack of hundreds of diaries from the time when she passionately believed that was the business to get into. Then there's the second factory from the time when she was going to get into another business entirely. Oh, and don't forget that expensive piece of machinery that never even got up and running, all because, by the time it arrived, the ardour had cooled and Ms Gadfly's enthusiasm was off on another tangent.

Lesson: This one is easy to solve. Don't discourage your Ms Gadfly tendencies – they're just your creative element firing and we absolutely don't want to lose that. However, there's nothing to be gained from trying to do lots of things at once. So have an ideas board, where each new passion can get written up. And there it must stay for a prescribed period – perhaps a month, perhaps just a couple of weeks – and until that time has expired you're not allowed to do anything about it. Don't worry, very few of those 'highly time-sensitive opportunities' you're fretting about are ever quite so time sensitive that you can't park them for a fortnight or two. And better to miss the boat on a few things and ensure that the ones you *do* run make it past the 'brilliant, absolutely brilliant' stage.

Common Pitfall Number Seven: Mr Angry

He is: oh dear, you can practically *see* Mr Angry just from his name. Quick to fly off the handle, he's always just a hair's breadth from getting all red-faced and shouty. Sometimes you can sort of see his point, when the whole world seems to be falling around his ears. At other times, however, he can get disproportionately mad for no apparent reason at all. It really is quite scary. And it means everyone tiptoes around him all the time and is terrified to speak their mind or take a chance, in case it doesn't work out.

Lesson: A lot is known about what may appear to be mysterious, unjustified anger. It is clear that it's driven by fear – fear of failure, fear of being found out, fear of losing. What's also clear is that it frequently presents as a reaction to high levels of stress and that it can become a habit. So, with all that in mind, if you find yourself displaying anger, it's important to take a good hard look at yourself and try and work out how you 'do' anger. Regard it, if you like, as an unwelcome skill – socially unhelpful, unlikely to get the right result, but a skill nonetheless. When did you first learn it? In what circumstances do you 'do' your anger? If you can spot the pattern, you'll start to learn a little about what causes it. And once you know *that*, you can start to understand what it is about yourself or about your circumstances that you're afraid of.

Common Pitfall Number Eight: Ms Anal Retentive
She is: the kind of girl who may quite possibly iron her underpants. She'd rather die than see an 'i' undotted or a 't' uncrossed. She's so busy getting everything absolutely 100 per cent perfectly lined up, square, completely right – that she misses the action.

Lesson: C'mon. Life's to be lived, sex should be messy and, even if you disagree with that, any business that spends too much time getting things right that don't really matter is going to die, admittedly leaving a very neat corpse but one just as dead. If you have a tendency to spend too much time where it's not productive, you need to address this. Your personal life (and your sex life) is entirely your own – though it is, we can reveal, the subject of a future book we're working on – but you have to remember that business is business. The classic rule was devised by a guy named Pareto, who – actually, no that's not true. For reasons we needn't detain you with, the Pareto Principle was actually propounded by someone whose name, messily, wasn't Pareto at all.[15] But that's not important right now. What *is* important is that the Pareto Principle states that 80 per cent of your profits

---

[15] It was Joseph Juran. We like the idea that Ms Anal Retentive would get very, *very* agitated and upset that the whole notion of effective effort should be named after someone other than the guy who came up with the idea.

come from 20 per cent of your sales and 80 per cent of your results come from 20 per cent of your effort.

Anyway, it all comes down to this: if you are an obsessively neat person, beware. More positively, be sure to channel that effort into areas of the business where it pays off and recognise that there are bound to be things that don't respond well to your, er, particular brand of tenacity (or 'pedantry' as others are no doubt bound to call it, when they're being polite).

Common Pitfall Number Nine: Mr Fingers

He is: the boss who has his fingers in the till all the time. He's not running a kosher business. When it suits him, he dips. He fails to see a distinction between the money that belongs to the business and the money that belongs to him. It is his company, his business – ergo (and you should always be suspicious when someone starts using Latin) what belongs to the business belongs to him. A moment's thought would reveal this to be the ridiculous notion that it is, but he's too busy for such reflection. His problem may be coke or gambling or an excessively high mortgage or a mistress or... well, whatever the hell his problem is, it doesn't really make any difference. If he's dipping his fingers into the company till, he's a sleazebag who can't be trusted and whose people, quite rightly, have no respect for him.

Lesson: Keep your fingers out of the till. Regard the money in the business as sacred and never, ever blur the boundary. The moment you do, you're headed down a road that can't take you to Happytown.

Common Pitfall Number Ten: Mr Hands

He is: unhealthily concerned with sex, to the extent that it damages not only his personal life but his business life, too. He hires on the basis of breast size and buys from the suppliers on the same basis. He cannot resist commenting on the physical attractiveness or otherwise of every employee and customer. He is always flirting and may well make women around him uncomfortable, though he's unlikely to be aware of this. He talks dirty too – filthy jokes, indecent emails, anecdotes about last night's (quite possibly invented) escapades. The Christmas party is an occasion for embarrassment, exposure or illicit liaison, and it takes months to live down. Of course, this is much more likely to be the case with a middle-aged man, who is naturally having a bit of a midlife crisis. Young men who are getting plenty actually don't spend all their time thinking about it when they're supposed to have their minds on other things.

Lesson: Let's leave aside the moral aspects of all this – the humiliated wife, the children who don't get to see too much of their old man. Instead let's just consider the financial and other costs to the business of all this distraction and misdirected energy. If the boss is thinking so much and so hard about The Wild Thing, that's all passion and mindspace that isn't going on the job in hand (er, as it were). The solution is to sort out one's private issues and get a grip, so to speak. The workplace really isn't the place for this stuff – especially if you're the boss. For one thing, you're setting a terrible example and your employees will rapidly work out where your priorities lie. If you're really more interested in getting into your secretary's pants than building a business, they'll spot that. And you'll get what you're looking for: trousers down, profits down.

So what?

So what does all that mean for your business?

Stay focused, that's what. Whatever your little weakness is – and it may or may not be one we've touched on above – keep it out of your business, and if you can't do that, minimise its impact as soon as you walk through that office door.

We're having a bit of fun with this, by the way (that's the kind of crazee cats we are!), but on a serious note, if there really is something weighing you down, think about getting some help – whether it be counselling, a life coach, business mentor or a long, long night at the local with a good friend. Better to get it straightened out, whatever it is, than let it get in the way of your business.

If you can keep yourself nice and on track and not all wobbly, then frankly, you'll be doing better than 90 per cent of small business owners out there. Repressing the wonky bits of your personality and becoming a better, more consistent player is instant competitive advantage. And who wouldn't like a bit of that?

CHAPTER EIGHTEEN

WHAT ARE YOU LIKE? THE NATURAL HISTORY OF THE ENTREPRENEUR

> **What surprised me? The applicability and value of my skills.** Peter Borg, Peter Borg & Associates

There is a strong streak of bloody-mindedness about an entrepreneur – a fierce desire to make decisions for oneself. Frankly, such people don't make terrific employees, for a fairly obvious reason: *they don't like being told what to do.*

What makes someone this way? It varies. Some are looking for that work/life balance we hear so much about and do so little to achieve. Talk to them, as we have, and the F-words (Flexibility, Freedom, F*** the boss) recur constantly:

> **'I have always been motivated by freedom and held the belief that working for someone was not the best way to generate cash. My first business was started when I was 17, but the next (current) was not for another 13 years. I ventured again to change the world. It is still a work in progress!'** Stuart Hayes, Starnext

> **'In my deepest psyche, I wanted to help small business owners because they are the backbone of any economy. They are the dreamers who make things happen.'** Eric de Diesbach, Platinum Advice

> **'I needed more flexibility to raise my family of three young children.'** Sarah Day, Day One Business Services

With others, the financial disaster of redundancy from the safety of Corporate World was reframed to present a valuable opportunity to make the move to self-employment:

'Redundancy from corporate life forced me to make a decision and working for myself seemed the ideal way to use my experience gained in the corporate world.' Robert Sampimon, Sampimon Business Solutions

'Lost a job at 60. Saw no opportunity to be hired. Tried to figure out what and how I could earn a living.' David Hollinger, Prime Business Group

Some just get heartily sick and tired of the politics that are common – and may even be universal and necessary – in corporate life. As one particularly eloquent entrepreneur put it:

'I got thoroughly sick and tired of the multinational corporate bullshit environment. These corporates are so inward focused it's frightening. More time is spent on internal proposals, motivations, reporting and arse-covering. Politics is rife and self-interest is like a cancer. Expat managers have only marble-polishing on their minds – and to hell with longer-term objectives. Strategy is a foreign concept.' John Shaw, Beachcroft Consulting

Marching to the beat of a different drum

For those of us who feel this way, what may be surprising is that others don't. Yet there is a suspicion that it's the entrepreneurial spirit, and not the corporate environment, that is the critical factor here. After all, there are millions and millions of people all over the world working within the belly of the corporate beast, and while many presumably do so only because they have no choice (or rather, that's how they perceive it), there are many, presumably more, who get along just fine.

Let's face it: we're just not very good at conforming, most of us. (Note: we say 'most of us,' because we're perfectly well aware that what we're about to say doesn't apply to everyone and may not apply to you. However, it does apply to some of us and we just haven't noticed it about ourselves yet. So at least read what's coming with an open mind and consider whether there's a streak of truth in it. If you're convinced there isn't, then that's fine. Just…read it first, is all.)

We, the entrepreneurs, are not made of the right stuff to survive, let alone thrive, in the corporate world. What do we mean? Well, think of it for a moment from the point of view of someone trying to run a business unit within a vast international corporate entity. On the one hand, there are the entirely legitimate demands from shareholders, who require their investment to turn a profit. They want the biggest return they can get and anything that reduces it – such as compliance costs, employee salaries, environmental concerns, taxation and customer demands – is an unwelcome cost: a necessary evil (and possibly not necessary). On the other hand, there are other stakeholders, such as the aforementioned customers and employees, whose interests are entirely otherwise. There may well be local interests to balance as well. Add in the particular agenda of the boss in question herself. The net result is likely to be a bit of a hotch-potch.

> It never ceases to amaze me how and why corporates are successful. They are, generally speaking, so inefficient and unproductive it beggars belief. Yet in spite of themselves they succeed. It must be sheer size and momentum in a lot of cases. But then again, history is littered with large companies that fail spectacularly. SMEs are the drivers of most economies. They are successful because of a person's passion, dream or vision. The tragedy is that as soon as the business becomes a threat, some corporate comes a long and buys it. And there it goes…swallowed up into another corporate – and with it all the passion, dreams and vision. Pity really. John Shaw, Beachcroft Consulting

Now throw another factor into the equation: *you*. Maybe you do not recognise the legitimacy of the pressures your boss is under. The share-holders can go take a running jump. The self-interested employees with their hidden and overt agendas are not worthy of your consideration. OK, so maybe the customers do have a point, and after all serving them is what this business is all about, isn't it? But as for all the rest of it, the politics and the whole rest of the nonsense, well, you just can't be doing with that, can you?

You like to think of yourself as the only honest person in the place. You're the grit in the oyster that makes the pearl. You tell it like it is. You have no hidden agenda and what you want is only for this organisation to achieve its potential, to focus on performance, to think about what the customer wants to buy rather than what the company wants to sell them.

Your boss finds you exasperating. You are the grit, it's true, but Corporate World is not an oyster but a machine, and grit produces not pearls but friction. You're impossible to keep on track. He probably even believes you when you say you mean well, although you have the most peculiar way of showing it. At the top of your game, you're the very best in the place – but the top of your game is all too rarely in evidence and getting rarer by the day. You're becoming High Maintenance.

> **'Why did I start my own business? I could not tolerate working for anyone else any longer.'** Stan Sweeney, Guidepost Strategies

> **'I was convinced that I could offer a far better service if I wasn't hampered by normal corporate constraints. I wanted to make my own decisions and achieve something myself. It is the ultimate responsibility, when you start your own business you are totally accountable and there is no one else to blame when things go wrong and no one else to take the credit for your achievements. Even if you have employees to whom you ultimately give credit, there is still room to pat yourself on the back for having made a great choice in employing them.'** Jo Rhodes-Lewis, Tangible Developments Ltd

Actually it makes little sense to ask whether it's the entrepreneurial spirit that's at fault, or the corporate environment itself. Both are fine in their own way – it's just they're like oil and water, chalk and cheese, Brown and Blair: *they just don't get along.*

Cry freedom

Closely allied to this is an unscratchable itch for freedom:

'**Free to decide city of residence, free to plan the working hours, independence for taking decisions, etc.**' Firdaus N. Kapadia, FNK Corporation

'**I started my own business because I saw the opportunity to design a lifestyle that would suit me best and to create the financial rewards equal to the effort I put in.**' Carl Gould, CMT International

'**[I had the] desire to work for myself.**' Garth Borgelt, Allsorts Consulting & Training

'**I wanted: 1) freedom to focus on the kind of work I like; 2) to build a great working relationship with a team of associates I respect and who keep me challenged and motivated; 3) the journey of discovery, variety of work and contexts, meaning that you learn something new every time as well as apply your existing skills.**' Françoise Garnier, Garnier Marketing Pty Ltd

'**I had the desire to take control of my career and escape the politics of corporate employment.**' David Jenkins, TDnJ Business Consulting

How much does this ring true for you? If you recognise this yearning with a shock, then it's likely that you have that same unscratchable itch – or rather, it's likely that it will always be unscratchable while you remain within the corporate structure. This is not certain, of course: it is absolutely possible to find yourself in a role with enough freedom to be able to do your job without getting caught up in all that political nonsense. But such situations are not common, and the wind can change with dismaying rapidity and blow away all your hard-earned freedom, leaving you and your people exposed and vulnerable.

'A corporate merger was forced on my company/division. I did not agree with the process and could not accept the offer to stay for moral/ethical reasons.' Carel Venter, Centre for Synergy Development

Being asked to execute (the word is chosen carefully) the plans of a new power within the organisation, be it a new owner or a new MD, is often more than can be stomached. This respondent, typical of many, was driven to leave and set up an independent business by:

'A desire to make a difference in the lives of others and control my destiny in the process.' Les Stuckey, A3 Consulting & Coaching

Whose life is it anyway?

And this is without even mentioning one of the most obvious factors of all: time. When you were a student you had little money and, so it seemed then, as much time as you wanted. Now, time is at a premium and…well, it would have felt like a lot of money back then, but it doesn't look like a whole lot now, especially when considering what you have to give to get it. Just the very act of getting to and from work, for instance, eats up a massive amount of your week – time that could be better spent with your family:

'I *hated* commuting and don't much like being stuck an office for 40 hours a week either…so I had to create the perfect job for myself…I mainly work from home.' Robert Hamilton-Jones, Business Advantage International

Another of our respondents describes being 'burnt out by travel' (Ashley Fernandes, Crossing Cultures).

Finally Mary Honan, from For Marketing Matters, sums up pretty much the whole shooting match as well as anyone – the frustrations of the corporate world, the redundancy, turning a disaster into an opportunity to pursue one's passions and address the life/work balance and the thrill of building one's own business. That's your cue Mary, take it away:

'I was laid off and leveraged the time to sit back and think about what I *really* wanted to do with my career and to balance my personal goals with my professional goals. I wanted to have more control over what work I did and when I did it and as a working mother, I wanted the flexibility of being available for my kids while working hard at building my own business.'

CHAPTER NINETEEN

WHERE IS ALL THIS GOING?

> There were some dark days initially, mainly due to questioning myself... uncertainty about how to build credibility, uncertainty about which business was right for me, uncertainty about which people to collaborate with. I think all the worst things were of my own making and once I realised that, it became a lot easier! Alison Richardson, Richardson Associates

Put down this book and, in a moment, think about your business venture for five minutes. (By now you should be used to our bossy instructions that you put down the book and think for a bit. And you don't *have* to. What are we going to do, come round and check up on you?) Consider what you expect it to look like in 12 months, three years, five years and nine years from now.

The things to think about are the same key elements we've been talking about all along:

- what **gets you up** in the morning
- you and your **lifestyle**
- your **product** or service
- your **customers** and market
- your **dream team** – the support around you

Will it all look exactly the way it does now, or will it change?

What are the top things you would like to see? Go on – in your not quite wildest dreams, how would you love your business look in, say, five years down the track? And what are the top things you expect to see?

Call this Vision A:

_____

_____

_____

_____

_____

Now, looking at how things have worked out so far, if you continued that pattern and curve, what do you think might _actually_ happen?
Let's call this Vision B:

_____

_____

_____

_____

_____

What is the gap between Vision A and Vision B? And what can you do about it?

_____

_____

_____

_____

_____

Chances are Vision A has you thinking about something like this: growth, expansion, occasional hiccup, challenges, ups and downs and always – we hope – onwards, upwards, bigger, better and more. Which is great, but it's a bit unstructured too and that's going to make it harder to achieve. As you know by now (assuming you haven't just flicked to the back in the hope of not having to read the whole book), it's always easier to achieve your goals when you plan them out.

This bit is hard work, by the way. For a start, you're looking into the future:

1. **It's hard to know when the growth will come**, when the challenges will come, and in what order.
2. Although you can very easily imagine that there will be challenges and setbacks and, you hope and pray, victories and successes, **it's virtually**

impossible to predict what is going to cause them and what type they'll be.

3. **You haven't got there yet**, so you don't know how it will all feel. You'll change along the way too, as will the business.

And although forecasting your future and planning what will happen is difficult, there are ways of taking a stab at it. For example, if you can learn from the experience of other start-ups to avoid making their mistakes, then you will, won't you? If you're going to go broke, at least it'd be nice to do so in a novel and interesting way no one's ever thought of before. (Only kidding.)

To grow or not to grow

There are two main forecasts you might have come up with for Vision A and Vision B. Let's have a look.

Situation stable

There is a lot more than you realise in running a small business. The first 12 months – nothing like I thought it would be. Had to evolve and change to stay alive. Richard Ferguson, Web Enhancer

Maybe you're not thinking about growth at all. Maybe you're pretty happy with things just the way they are now, or will be in a year or two. You, maybe with a colleague or two, doing your business, probably working from home still, making a decent living wage and hopefully tucking a bit away. That's you sorted.

Don't let anyone feel there's anything wrong with that as a goal, either. The vast majority of small businesses work like that; they find their size (often a one-person band) and stick to it. We don't all have to be Sir Richard, after all. God forbid, what with the teeth and that annoying habit of upending ladies when there are cameras.

But looking to the future, it's good to remember that stability still means change too. Your market and customers will change and, at some level, you'll need to maintain pace just to stay still.

Where will that change come from? A few key areas:

- **your competitors** will grow/shrink and new competitors will enter your market, doing things a bit differently, a bit faster, a bit cheaper;

- **your customers** will get older and new ones will come in with different expectations – or they won't come at all, which is worse;

- **new technologies** will update how things work;

- **new ideas** will become fashionable and in demand.

So while we don't know how it will work out, what we do know is that if you're still doing business in five or ten years with the same offerings you're taking to market now, you may find it gets harder and harder as you go along instead of easier and easier. Which will mean you'll need to adjust your business accordingly (or just work harder and harder to scrape a living, which doesn't sound like much fun).

Think of the printing industry, for example. Print managers and buyers were trundling along quite happily, thank you very much. Then the digital world arrived and, before you know it, everyone can print their own stuff on a big photocopier and make it look professional. Graphic design, ditto.

Maybe you bought a gym a few years ago (no, we know you didn't – it's just an example). The recent trend for personal training has seen all your customers suddenly go jogging round the park with their personal trainer rather than working out back at Sweat Central. Gym owners who were smart hired personal trainers to work from their premises; gym owners who weren't, didn't – and lost out.

So you'll need to stay on top of what's happening in your industry and adjust if you have to. Like this:

- **All that stuff we said before** about networking, reading industry mags and so on? That's going to continue to apply, even if you think you know it all now.

- **Review your business regularly**; check you are still working towards your goals and create new goals if needed.

- Keep an eye on your **competition**.

- **Listen to your customers!** They won't tell you what they want, but they will vote with their feet or wallets. If you start to notice trends that leave you out in the cold, act.

Even if stability is what you want, you need to be open to change if it comes along, and knowing enough about what's in demand to make the right decisions will certainly help secure your future.

Situation growth

Where possible, try to start the business with adequate capital – this increases your chances of succeeding and also means you can grow much quicker. Robert Hamilton-Jones, Business Advantage International

You're looking for the big time. You want serious staff, a serious office, maybe branches and franchises rolling out your product or method worldwide.

How?

Probably not overnight, unless you have some snappy product that will take the world by storm (Mousetrap 2.0, anyone?). Even then, to take advantage you need a stable, secure business that's throwing off a lot of cash.

If you want to grow your business you'll need:

- **more staff for all that work** – sales and marketing, technical help, financial people, operations: you'll have to identify the gaps and hire in what's required;

- **more premises** – bigger and better than where you've started out… somewhere to put the staff for a start. Now you're no longer a micro-business, you're an SME. But what happened to your nimble, fleet-of-foot, overhead-free existence?;

- **more products/services** – the same thing you've been rolling out probably won't be enough to help you grow as much as you'd like;

- **more market channels** – a wider base of customers, whether that be by varying the product to reach up and down the demographic spread (reaching into mass markets, for example, instead of the boutique end of the market you've been dealing with) or by export, perhaps, with all the challenges and competition that comes with it;

- **more and better systems and communications** – your old PC running Excel won't cut it for a proper customer database. Systems and procedures that worked so well for a small business just won't work for something so much bigger. Finding solutions for these issues may be what you spend your day-to-day on, rather than scouring for customers and quoting on jobs; you have staff who do that now. But once you find the new shape of your business, you'll make it more efficient, more robust and more capable of expanding than it was before;

- **being clever about your business model** – and we're not just talking about being a sole trader or a company, though you might need to reconsider that too (we did, after a couple of years). You'll need to let go a bit, to delegate. Otherwise you'll turn into one of those micro-managing psychobosses spying on staff and trying to catch them signing out a second biro before they've used up the first one. Remind yourself to trust in the professionalism of the staff you've hired to make the right decisions.

That's a lot of more. It's far from easy – setting yourself up for growth, making the kind of hard-nosed and astute business decisions you know you need to make, without turning into one of the very bosses who made you decide to leave Corporate World in the first place!

The path ahead

It's natural to assume that once you're through the first year or two, the business will progress ultra-smoothly and you'll live happily ever after. After all, the first bit is where it's really hard, right? You're finding your market and your structure and building up a customer base and all that. Once you've got that sorted, work will flow in and you'll never have to worry about a thing again. Surely?

Oh dear.

Whether large or small and growing or staying stable in size, your business won't necessarily have a smooth road ahead. All businesses – well if not all, then certainly the great majority of them – tend to go through phases as they grow older: times when things are good and times when everything is a bit rocky too.

If we can draw on a somewhat cheesy analogy, think of it as going for a long car trip. A very, very, very, very long car trip. We're not just popping up to Yorkshire to see Aunty Doris; we're driving around Australia.

The prep comes first – planning, packing, swearing at the kids to get moving, heading off and wondering how the other people, like the neighbours, seem to manage just to jump in the car and go.

Once you're on the road, you go for ages and it's a fun ride, but then you start needing to stop and make adjustments. For a start, the usual pitstops such as petrol, servicing and natural breaks. Then your fanbelt goes when you're in the middle of nowhere and you have to tie it together with a pair of tights. Then you have a blissful period of uninterrupted sight-seeing (albeit *sans* tights), where life is perfect. Then you leave one of the kids at the caravan park and, after thinking it over for a minute, decide you do have to drive 20 miles back. Then you camp underneath the stars and everything is good. Then your Sat Nav gets stolen and you start to wonder if this was a good idea in the first place or if it would be better to go back to your normal life – it's not as exciting, but you know where everything is and what time you're supposed to get up in the morning.

Your business will be like that. It won't be a smooth trip – not the entire way, anyway. And some days you'll love it and others you will want *out*. Running your own business may, on the whole, beat the alternative, but we won't pretend it's sunshine and roses all the way.

But at least once you're aware that there will be bumps on the road, you won't be surprised when they come along and you can employ strategies to minimise problems and speed your way along.

Your business is likely to evolve through three different phases:

Phase One: the starting bit

This is likely to take a couple of years, give or take. You're working through your first client meeting, your first sale, the first bank deposit or cheque (yay!). You're learning new things every day and probably making mistakes every day too. Not surprisingly, you grab at any opportunity for work. Cash flow is so critical you don't have any choice. Your business will probably be very up and down, with huge bursts of work required, where you are at it 20 hours a day and have to hire in sub-contractors, and then quiet periods where despair hits and you find yourself desperately cold calling and letter-box dropping and wondering if you've made the right decision.

Your biggest worry, almost certainly, will be cash – or, more accurately, the lack of it. Your bank account will be down to the dregs more times than you'll have hot dinners, and unless you can bring in the next sale, there's no guarantee you won't slip into the red, or worse.

Remember all that stuff we did in Chapter 2 about personality styles? If you're someone who thrives on a challenge and hard work and is endlessly optimistic, this may not faze you at all. On the other hand, if security and stability are big on your list, all this turmoil may make your motivation go up and down. **This is why a lot of start-ups fail**, by the way – not because they don't have the right potential and not because the people are not hard workers or clever, but because they just don't like the chaos of these early days.

A lot of businesses start out well and then get a bit off course. When you're so busy running your things, it's hard to remember to stop and assess your business to make sure you're driving it in the right direction. Here are some **top tips to get you through the first few years**:

- **Stop.** Every six months in the first couple of years, and every year after that, do a business health check. Work your way through this book again;

go back to basics. Are you still heading where you want to go? Are you getting closer to your goals? If not, why not and what can you do about it?

- **It's easy to want to be all things to all people.** If you target your product and your market, you'll get better work – more enjoyable, better paid.

- **Remember to focus on your customer, not your product.** Who is your ideal customer? What do they want? How can you amend your product or service to get more business in?

- **Get practical with your goal setting.** Rather than setting massive goals that set you up for failure, settle for modest ones that will encourage you to go on. After all, it's true that success breeds success. (Just yesterday, Steve spoke to a guy who was in the very first flush of developing his business. Asked to set a goal for his first year, he said he was aiming for a million in turnover and three hundred thousand in profits. Ouch! It could happen, of course, and that would be wonderful. But very, very few businesses find such an opportunity so fast, especially if they are manufacturing businesses being set up by a sole individual with no capital behind them. Give yourself a chance of beating your target. Set your standards high and your goals a little lower.)

- **Create an information base** to help your decision-making. Your financial data will tell you how much you're making in terms of sales – and it can tell you how much each customer is spending; how much each market segment is spending; how efficiently (profitably) you're delivering your product to them; which are your most profitable products and which has most potential. Interrogate your figures and you can see where your business needs to go, and how it can make the most of the opportunities that arise.

- **Build a rolling programme of marketing.** It's very easy only to do business development when things are slow and there's spare time; or only when things are going very well and there's spare cash. Instead, find ways of promoting your business that don't depend on money or time. For example, call ten prospects each and every week, no matter what, regardless of whether business is good or bad. Of course, you can increase things when you have capacity and scale them back when no one has a moment to scratch themselves – but you need to make sure there is a constant tick, tick, tick of activity to keep a constant flow of business coming in.

Then, because you're smart and you've read this book and put the hard work in and done lots of other things that give you an advantage over other start-ups, you should see your business really settle in and start to thrive.

Phase Two: you hit your stride

You might not even notice when you hit your stride – it will just happen. Probably around the three year mark, maybe sooner or a bit later, you'll suddenly realise that you're no longer living in crisis every second of every day. Cash flow starts to ease up, just a little. Work starts to even out. You start to feel confidence in your ability to do this thing. When you don't win the business, you don't wake up at 5 a.m. wondering what went wrong; you just accept it goes that way sometimes. But you win more of the business anyway, because you've applied the experiences of the early days and got better at that bit. You even find yourself able to say 'no' occasionally to work you're offered that you know isn't quite right for your business. And you stop worrying about your quotes and if you're charging too much or not enough. That's the price and they can use you or not use you; no worries.

So now you're settling in for the long haul. But just when you fondly imagine you have it all worked out, it throws an absolute wobbly and scares the living daylights out of you. Suddenly the lid flies off and out come all kinds of problems and difficulties you never expected. (Except that you will expect them, because you've already been tipped off that they're likely to happen.)

Success can be scary, just because success often means change. You'll need to manage that process of change. So here are some tips for the ongoing future and success of your business:

- There will come a point when **the business doesn't quite mean everything** to you any more. There is, in fact, a little distance between you and it. This comes as quite a shock and can even lead some business owners to feel a little lost, as they search for their next big challenge. Celebrate when you reach your goals; then set new goals!

- If you've been living on a shoestring and working huge hours for years, **success may take you by surprise**. There will come a point when it's OK to step back a bit; when you can draw back from the business what you've been putting in all these years (whether it's cash or time or both).

- Just because something worked for you back then – when you started, when you were finding your feet – **doesn't mean it's the right solution** now that your business is thriving and established.

Phase Three: next stop?

Where to, guv'nor? Well, wherever you want to go, really:

- Eventually, you might want to think about a **succession plan**. There will come a time when you won't be willing and able to do this any more. And if you want to see your business continue on and be healthy, you'll need someone else to take over the reins, whether it be staff or family – someone who knows how it works, why it is successful and has some ideas for new directions too.

- If you got into this whole thing for a particular reason, that might change and the business might hit a point where it's **not right for you**. A lot of women work for themselves while the kids are young, for example, but then choose to head back to the reliable income and paid holidays of Corporate World as the little darlings become more independent. Nothing wrong with that. Reassessing your needs doesn't mean you're not committed to your business. And if the answer is that it's time to do something different, then move on!

- Let us leave you with this thought: the real money in small business is if you grow it to the point where you can sell up. There, we've finally said it, right at the end, when it's likely to make the most impact. We'll say it again: **you make your big bucks on the way out**. Or rather, that's your best opportunity. Amazingly, though, the great majority of businesses never actually cash in. Either the proprietor locks the door and walks away, or at best sells it for a fraction of the price it's worth – all because no thought was given to how to cash in. The subject of this book hasn't been how to sell your business, but rather how to start it. However, if there's only one thing you take away from your time with us, then (a) you clearly weren't paying attention and (b) if that thing is only this, that business owners make their real money when they sell, then at least you've taken away the single most valuable point in the whole book.

And now...it's up to you. Best of luck. Strap yourself in for the ride of your life!

INDEX